Word Fill-In Puzzles

Fill In Puzzle Book, 110 Puzzles: Vol. 1

by John Oga

Word Fill- In Puzzles

**Fill In Puzzle
Book,
110 Puzzles: Vol. 1**

ISBN-13: 978-1539592808

Table of Contents

Puzzles

1

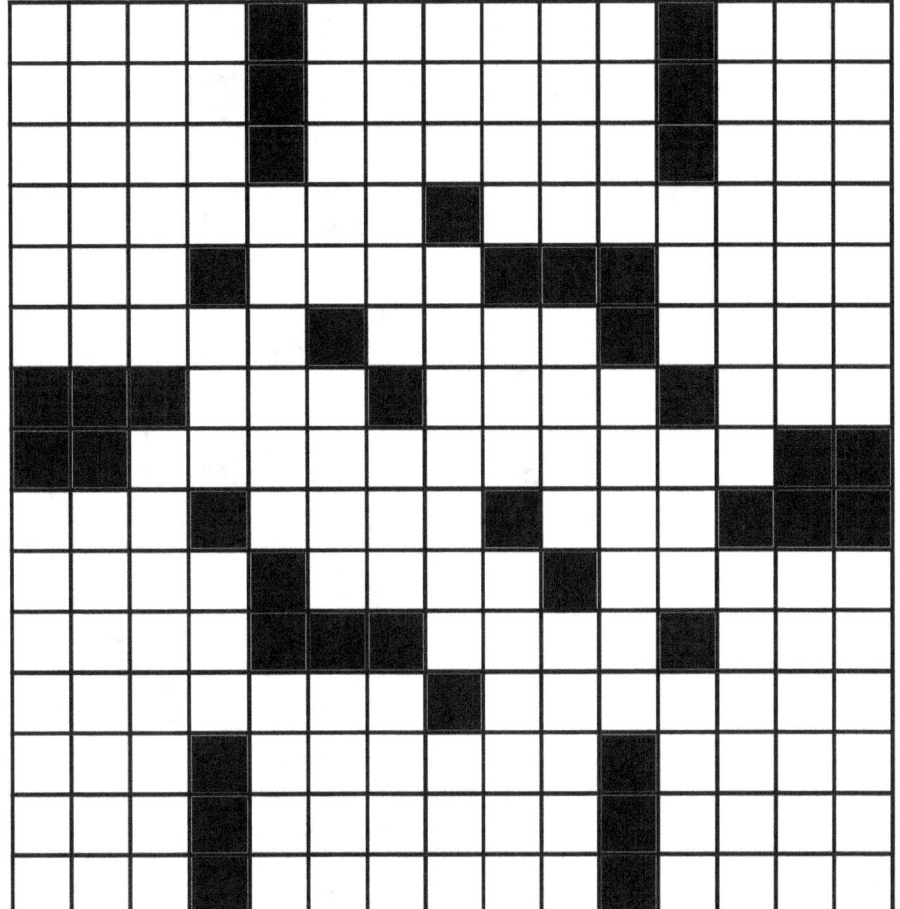

3 Letter
Ape
Apt
Ate
Dip
Err
Gel
Hem
Ill
Lop
Lye
Moo
Oar
Pas
Per
Pit
Row
Rue
Sly
Tat
The

4 Letter
Abed
Able
Ajar
Bate
Bran
Elan
Else
Fern
Hail
Hone
Idle
Idol
Loam
Lump
Prop
Push
Rest

Rime
Sari
Soda
Stow
Take
Toga
Unto
Weft
Yo-yo

5 Letter
Cleat
Ratty
Rigid
Utter

6 Letter
Amount
Annals
Bought
Employ
Eureka
Gneiss
Inhale
Lament
Litany
Public
Rather
Redden
Stable
Techno
Tribal
Unroll

7 Letter
Apropos
Catbird
Ease off
Iron Age
Letting
Lobelia
Overall
Program
Trivial

8 Letter
Demijohn
Geometry

11 Letter
Gentlewoman

2

3 Letter
Ark
Bra
Can
Cat
Gnu
Hit
Inn
Ism
Key
Let
Man
Mat
Met
Sea
Ski
USA
Who

4 Letter
Ages
Arch
Area
Aunt
Cast
Coin
Cult
Espy
Hind
Hint
Onto
Open
Path
Rags
Same
Scar
Stem
Sure
Than
Thou
User
Wash

5 Letter
Chant
Elope
Frame
Groan
Madam
Penal
Renal
Stone
Traps

6 Letter
Albino
Anoint
Arched
Elicit
Encore
Fresco
Genera
German
Litter
Orator
Pomade
Reckon
Redden
Stable
Stolid
Waiter

7 Letter
Concede
Halogen
Ice pack
Notelet
Outrank
Piteous

8 Letter
Analogue
Honorary
Untimely
Whitecap

10 Letter
Economical
Out on a limb

3

3 Letter
Cue
Dan
Hew
Ira
Oca
Odd
Pet
PTA
Pul
Run
Sea
Tea

4 Letter
Aria
Deed
Edgy
Else
Ever
Flaw
G-man
Hods
Idol
Knee
Mean
Noll
Parr
Reel
Sari
Secs

5 Letter
Afire
Aloha
Apron
Arête
Arose
Carib
Easel
Eliot
Loath
Ratio
Slang
Stela
Tesla
Testy
Tetra
Topee

6 Letter
Anodal
Apexes
Betake
Escarp
Kidney
Remade

7 Letter
Exposit
Leucine
Matures
Nymphet
Odonata
Reel off
Riposte
Roe deer
Rwandan

Tiniest
Trucker
Wassail

8 Letter
Ectoderm
Laggards
Moderate
Stellate

9 Letter
Atonement
Cadaveric
Desalting
Rhodopsin

4

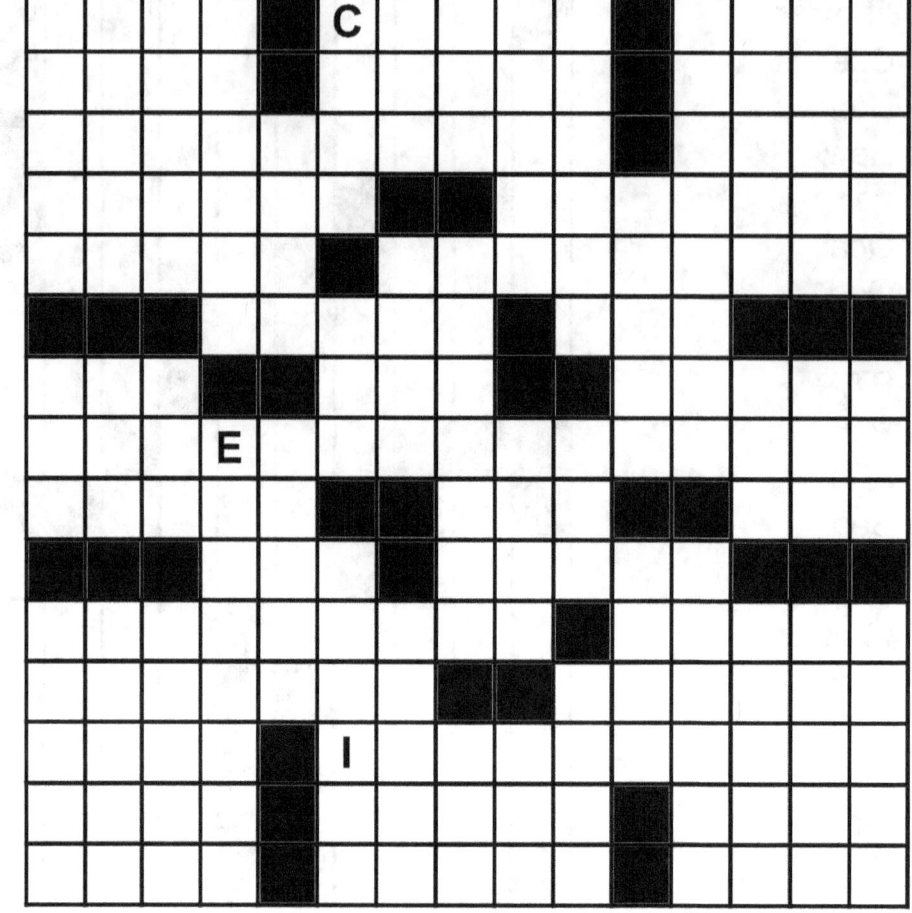

3 Letter
Ear
Era
Ere
Err
Inn
Its
Ode
One
Ova
Rut
She
Tar
Tea
The
Tit
Too
Tug
Tut

4 Letter
Anon
Bite
Clog
Clot
Corn
Cute
Even
Fish
Gala
Hour
Idea
Iron
Pith
Reed
Type
Ward

5 Letter
Alive
Caste
Child
Circa
Corps
Dealt
Drool
Edict
Enemy
Geese
Genie
Inure
Levee
Loner
Outgo
Ovule
Plebe
Ratio
Rehab
Sinus
Surly
Tenth
Total
Trait
Trend
Troop

6 Letter
Enlist
Feeler
Legman
Seduce
Teeter
Tremor

7 Letter
Buckram
Durable
Rosette

8 Letter
Backseat
Estrange

9 Letter
Estranged
Precisely

10 Letter
Initiative
Integrated

15 Letter
Under the
weather

5

3 Letter
Bra
Ear
Has
Kin
Lei
Opt
Rat
Son
Ten
War
Was
Yes

4 Letter
Agar
Airy
Also
Alto
Ante
Apse
Area
Band
Dead
Deep
Ease
Even
Gala
Ibis
Inch
Isle
Lees
List
Mine
Note
Papa
Read
Seer
Slat
Soar
Spew
Spin
Stow
Twit
Yelp

5 Letter
Adman
Aisle
Alter
Arbor
Atlas
Beryl
Bract
Caste
Deity
Easel
Event
Inlet
Media
Merit
Moire
Needy
Piste
React
Seine
Spent
Woody

6 Letter
Ambush
Ascent
Ferret
Fester
Floral
Nicety
Pierce
Smirch

7 Letter
Satiate

9 Letter
Apartment
Attenuate
Blood heat
Fair trade

11 Letter
Kind-hearted
Tea-strainer

6

3 Letter
Ant
DNA
Eel
Key
Nip
The
Too
UFO

4 Letter
Aeon
Army
Beta
Crib
Espy
Fino
Goad
Hemp
Lode
Lost
Mass
Meal
Nice
Ogre
Opal
Oral
Perk
Purl
Rang
Reel
Rile
Scab
Sera
Slot
Tact
Tray
Tsar
Undo

5 Letter
Adore
Afire
Amass
Arise
Armed
Brook
Carom
Curia
Dirge
Eagle
Empty
End on
Entry
Epoch
Glare
Hairy
Hyper

Leave
Loose
Moral
Nadir
Prone
Radar
Rebel
Recap
Salsa
Spawn
Traps
Wield
Yemen

6 Letter
Rancor
Sleeve

7 Letter
Dribble
Synergy

8 Letter
Baseball
Gene pool

11 Letter
Aides-de-camp
Loop-the-loop

12 Letter
Assembly line
Palette knife

7

3 Letter
Age
All
Apt
Are
Ate
Bee
Dew
Egg
Ego
Ere
Err
Ice
Ire
Lea
Lei
Not
Rat
Roe
Sat
Sit
Sty

4 Letter
Aver
Dare
Epic
Gear
Gout
Gram
Hale
Halo
Hone
Idea
Imam
Lama
Lira
Loll
Mice
Mote
Pier
Real
Reel
Rent
Ship
Slat

5 Letter
Abbot
Adios
Alarm
Algal
Allot
Alter
Arbor
Elope
Erect
Erupt
Geese
Later
Loner
Media
Penne
Plebe
Set in
Stave
Teeny
Title
Tweet
Viola

6 Letter
Caliph
Rather
Reamer
Tomtit

7 Letter
Tensile
Voltaic

8 Letter
Placenta
Stage set

9 Letter
Enteritis
Table wine

13 Letter
Alpha particle
Wheeler dealer

15 Letter
Transliteration

8

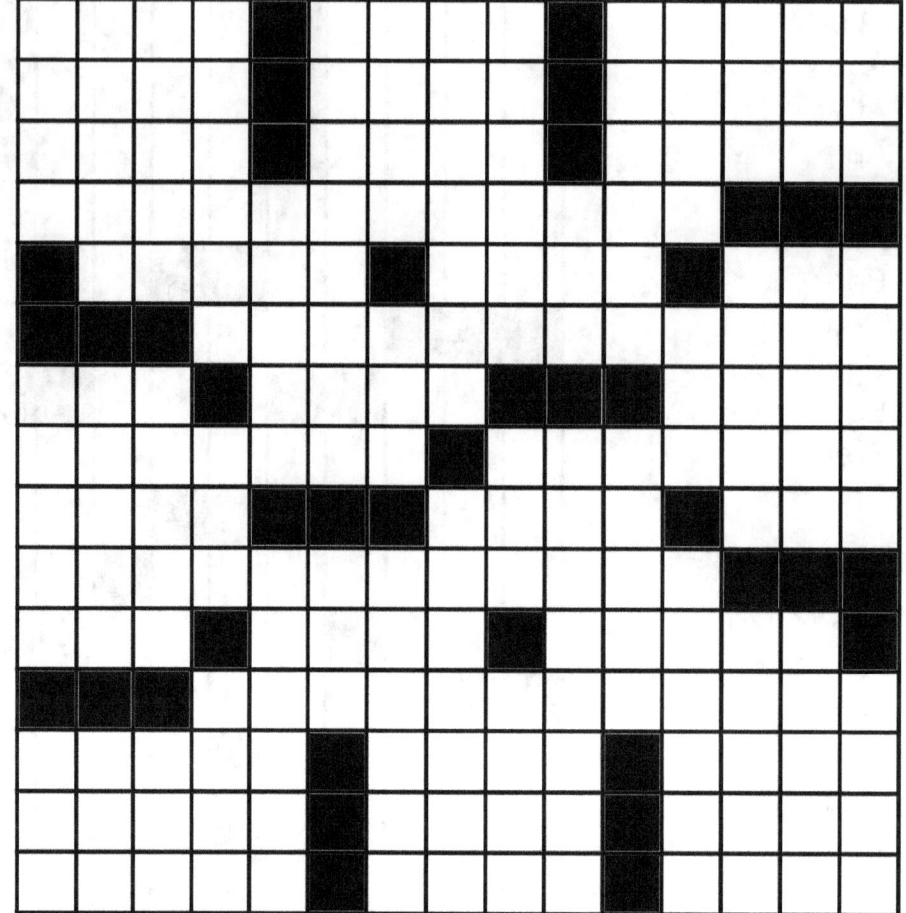

3 Letter
Ale
Asp
Bra
Cam
DNA
Egg
Err
Her
Lay
Per
Pet
Sea
Sly
Spa
Sun
Vat

4 Letter
Ache
Agar
Apex
Axle
Dire
Duet
East
Echo
Hide
Knee
Mire
Note
Rant
Rave
Reek
Reel
Rout
Sage
Sari
Sell
Stir
Taco
Toad
Tone

5 Letter
Ad-lib
Apart
Aster
Atone
Betel
Ethos
Étude
Expel
Genre
Giddy
Glare
Grill
Moral
Pasha
Payee
Rehab
Renew
Snarl
Snoop
Tenor

6 Letter
Edible
Extent
Pegleg
Retail
Teeter
Thanks

7 Letter
Corrode
Insider
Rat race
Triplet

8 Letter
Overlook
Steerage

12 Letter
Irremediable
Mineral water
Old Testament
Travel agents

9

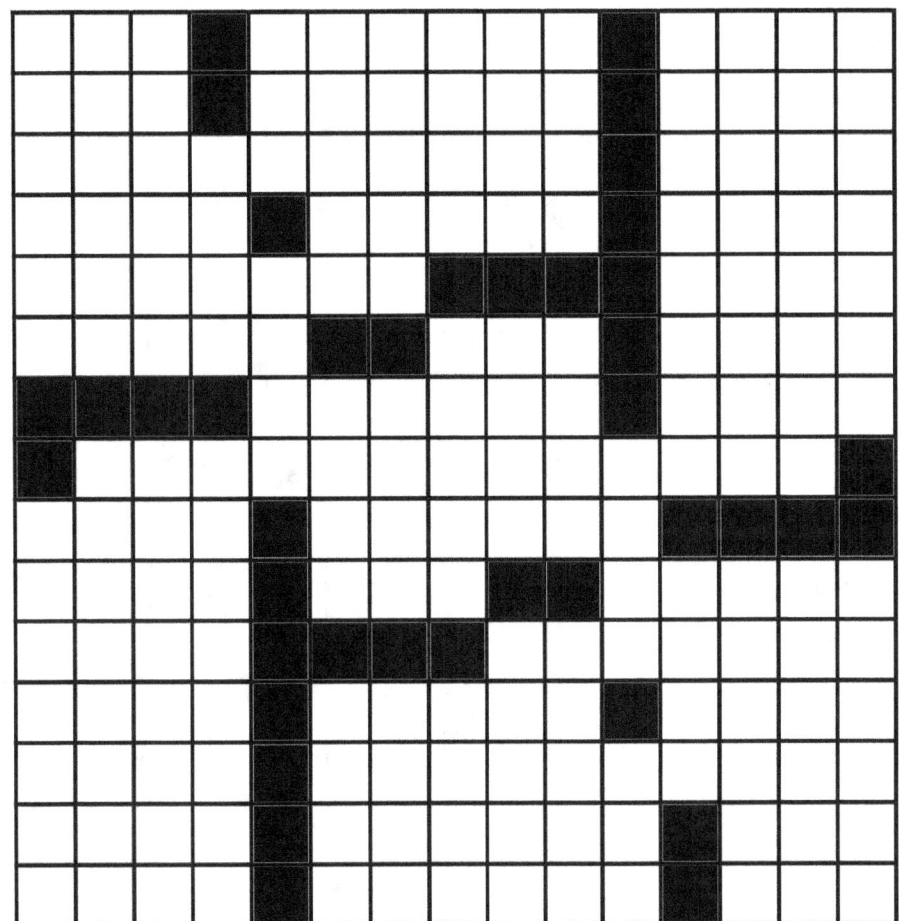

3 Letter
Ani
Ape
Dec
Ewe
Its
Per
Say
Spa

4 Letter
Aden
Ante
A-one
Arco
Area
Aryl
As if
Asks
Barb
Clam
Craw
Et al
Frit
Gage
Gene
Here
Isle
Jean
Knew
Lane
Mira
Nape
Need
Omen
Oval
Pool
Root
Snag
Some
Tape

5 Letter
Agist
Astir
Biped
Erode
Frown
Helms
Lethe
Payee
Shove

6 Letter
Alpaca
Anchor
Cicero
Day off
Enamor
Feeder
Iberis
Impede
Pavlov
Pearls
Sonata
Tressy

7 Letter
Belabor
Foresee
Harijan
Tenable

8 Letter
Areolate
Flambeau
Inerrant
Kerosene
Neatened
Radiator

10 Letter
Soap operas
Yackety-yak

13 Letter
Kangaroo court

10

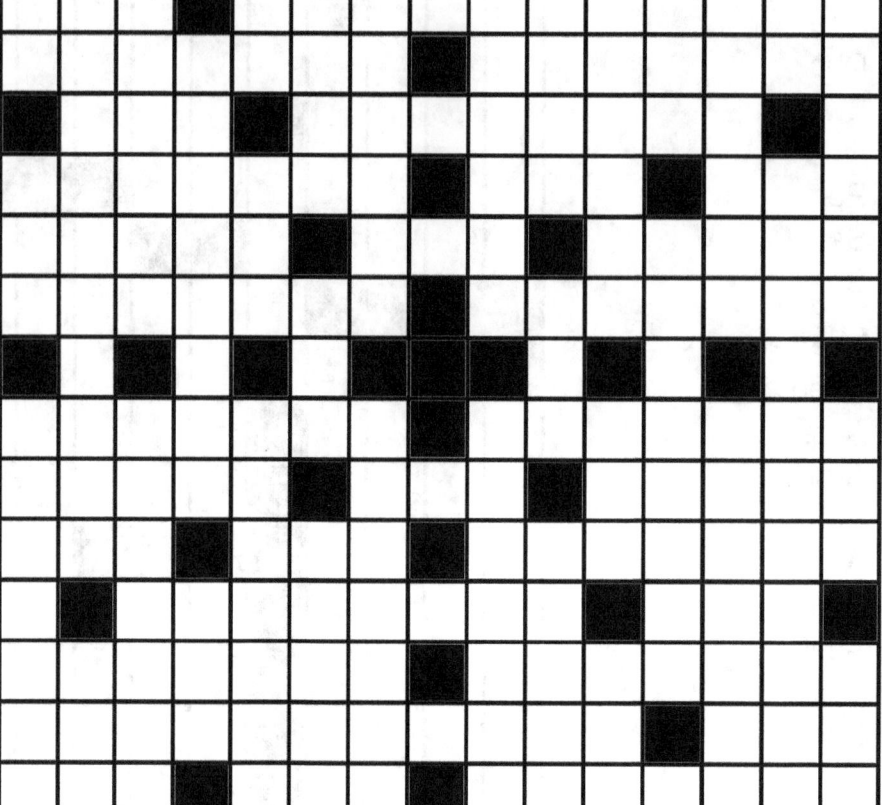

3 Letter
Ala
Asp
Ate
ATM
Ave
Dos
Ear
E'en
Emu
Eon
Etc
Far
Huh
Lap
Meg
Oat
One
Opt
Par
Red
REM
Sob
Tar
Ted
Tel
Too
Ups
Urn

5 Letter
Acrid
Noose
Obese
On air
Sarah
Slate
Steep
Those

7 Letter
Aspired
Attempt
Credits
Crouton
Demotes
Distend
Elation
Eternal
Fine art
Ironist
Manages
Partita
Rampart
Rereads
Rhubarb
Serener
Spotter

Stratus
Surinam
Terrine
Torpedo
Tramcar
Trapper
Uncross

8 Letter
Complied
East side
Panorama
Thesauri

11 Letter
Attributive
Dar es Salaam
Lie detector
Naphthalene

11

3 Letter
Age
Ail
Ape
Asp
Cha
Emu
Fix
Foe
Ill

4 Letter
Alas
Anti
Apex
Area
Aria
Bali
Boat
Cage
Coco
Coin
Cole
Conn
Crap
Crux
Deaf
Duel
Echo
Else
Emit
Euro
Exes
Guru
Half
Hall
Icon
Lend
Moan
Odor
Ogre
Oink
Oops
Oreo
Ouch

Pics
Pile
Read
Redo
Rial
Slit
Trap

5 Letter
Ate up
Congo
Darer
Drake
Enema
Ethos
Euros
Iliad
Optic
Pauli
Pests

6 Letter
Cloche
Dicker
E-books
Icicle
Nettle
Octave
Rapier
Recoup
Secret
Spouse
Strove
Vox pop

7 Letter
Envious
Home run

9 Letter
Argonauts
Re-examine

12 Letter
Cause célèbre
Telepresence

12

3 Letter
Daw
Dye
Ivy
Lei
Moo
Oca
Top
Two

4 Letter
Acme
Alky
Ally
Anoa
Bach
Bane
Ciao
Earn
Ebbs
Echo
Et al
Euro
Into
Laid
Lean
Noon
Nope
Odes
Ohms
Oreo
Pike
Road
Root
Rope
Send
Shoe
Star
Step
Tarn

Tarp
Whys
Wing

5 Letter
Ascot
Decoy
Diary
Diode
Enter
Enure
Erred
Evert
Learn
Olive
Oread
Purse
Rerun

Ruses
Suave
Unsay
Verne
Vroom

6 Letter
Ceased
Heaved
Ocular
Reject
Renoir
Revert
Smarmy
Tortes
Unease
Uneasy

7 Letter
In order
Relearn

8 Letter
Baroness
Spaniels

9 Letter
Broad jump
Dartmouth

12 Letter
Heartstrings
Rapid transit

13

3 Letter
Aah
Bra
Cod
Egg
Era
Fun
Inn
Lit
Lot
NBC
Orb
Ore
Out
Rag
Spa
Tan
Tao
Tar

4 Letter
Ados
Ajar
Asks
Brio
Claw
Crop
Ends
Erin
Ides
Iota
Kava
Kurd
Lava
Levi
Lieu
Lyra
Odin
Oval
Raja
Rave
Sire
Sirs
Tang
Thee
Tied
Tsar
Urge
Utah
Veda
Yous

5 Letter
After
Astir
Attar
Blood
Easel
Eight
Helot
Levin
Liana
Prong
Route
Shelf
Stats
Tufts

6 Letter
Angina
Earlap
Eighth
Gaiety
Parkas
Reheat
Relief
Tangos

7 Letter
Alpines
Aureole
Hoarder
Key ring

11 Letter
Flight decks
Second sight

12 Letter
Irreversible
Walkie-talkie

14

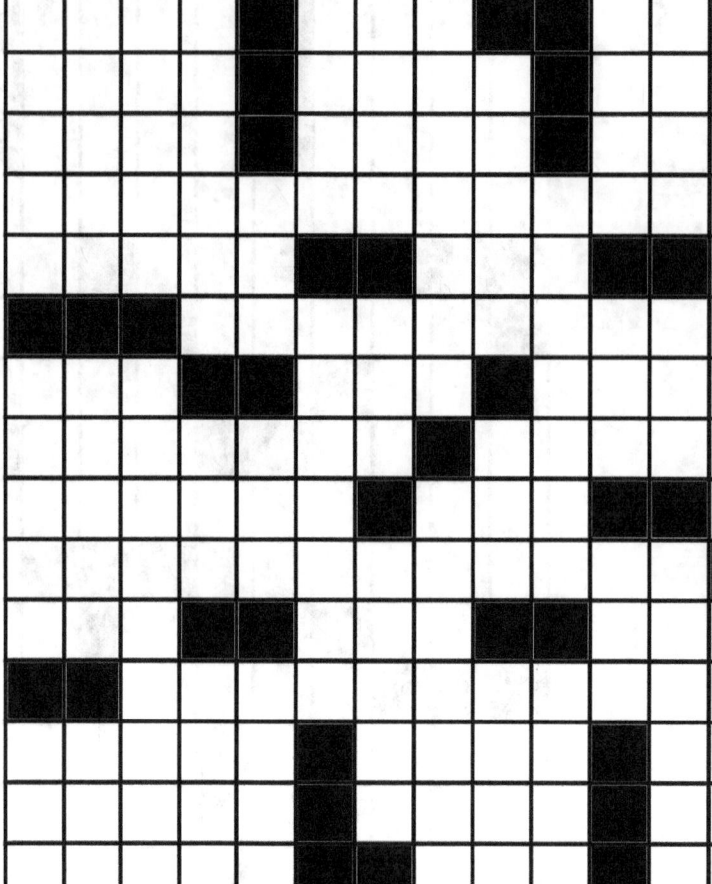

3 Letter
Aft
All
Ana
Bin
CIA
Cue
E'en
Eta
Goo
Ilk
Keg
Mat
Not
Owe
Pap
Pen
Reg
Sly
Tee
Use
Vet
Zee

4 Letter
Agog
Apse
Army
Dyer
Edda
Egis
Grab
Laic
Lewd
Lira
Melt
Menu
No-go
Plea
Roar

Slim
Tail
USSR

5 Letter
Agora
Alibi
Ankle
Arson
E-mail
Fatso
Gluts
Inlet
Oscar
Panel
Pasta
Peril
Ragga

Rishi
Sinew
Snide
Sober
Swank
Toady
Tsars

6 Letter
Bailed
Barren
Galoot
Pueblo

7 Letter
Amongst
Phenols
Reaping
Restful
Tighten
Ziegler

9 Letter
Golf links
Irascible

12 Letter
Gift of the gab
Nerve-racking

13 Letter
Implantations
Thoroughbreds

15

4 Letter
Ages
Alee
Ante
Crap
Edam
Espy
Hiss
Lees
Lens
Note
Ones
Ring
Rove
Tarp
Trap
True
Viol
Woad

5 Letter
Brest
Death
Ester
Nerve
Pries
Reads
Rosin
Seder
Slubs
Spars
Spawn
Stair
Steep
Tromp

7 Letter
At times
Atacama
Bipolar
Enraged
Hitters
Insider
Isthmus
Ménages
Nowhere
Operate
Overawe
Passado
Platoon
Pretest
Program
Proverb
Ravener
Reamers
Restate
Restore
Slender
Snorers
Step-ins
Strophe
Tanager
Ten-spot
Thalers
Toccata
Upstate
Wariest

9 Letter
Northwest
Steelyard

3 Letter

Ani
E'en
Elk
Gnu
Lac
Max
Neb
Net
Pol
Red
Sum
Tao
Use
Woo

4 Letter

Emir
Itch
Lava
Menu
Neve
Oast
Spur
Swob
Thai
Tsar
USPS
Visa

5 Letter

Abets
Alone
Bazar
Comic
Eaves
Erred
Folia
Iowan
Loath
Masai
Mauls
Monte

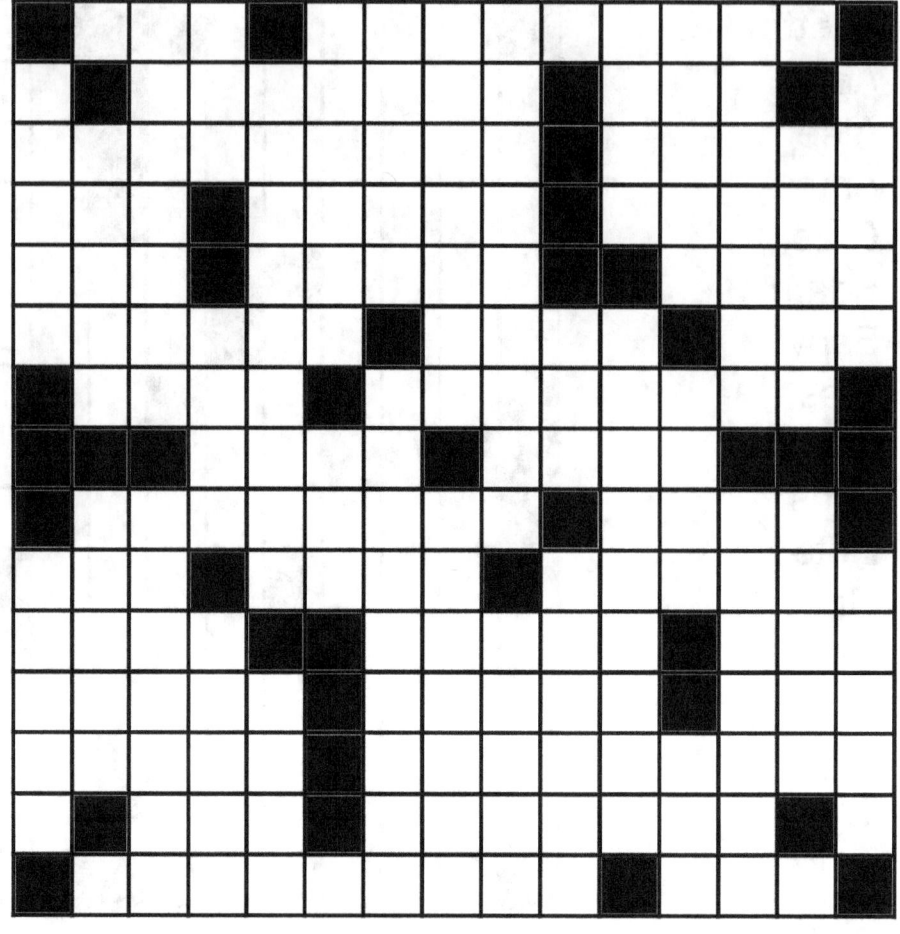

Mumps
Owner
Pin-up
React
Rural
Sibyl
Slung
Tenet

6 Letter

Sculpt
Singes
Snipes
To boot

7 Letter

At a time
Expunge
Intense
Mahouts
Non-zero
Ominous
Prolong
Spaniel

8 Letter

Mea culpa
Mementos

9 Letter

Begrudges
Bric-a-brac
Congruity
Half-price
Ischaemia
Malic acid
Traipsing
Unconcern

17

3 Letter
Ads
Alb
Bey
Ego
Fee
Lie
LSD
Res
Try
Urn

4 Letter
Acai
Acid
Acts
Anti
Bola
Deny
Ding
Erie
Icon
Omen
Rags
Safe
Sect
Slit

5 Letter
Angst
Count
Epoxy
Heels
Reply
Seems
Smash
Stead
Trews

6 Letter
Abrupt
Resend

7 Letter
Abilene
Abridge
Baptise
Blondes
Deep red
Entitle
Erelong
Fibulae
Gainful
Locoism
Martini
Nereids
Open-air

Promote
Sisters
Splints
Stabled
Stencil
Systole
Telexes
Terrier
Twinset
Up to par

8 Letter
Divagate
Paprikas

9 Letter
Albacores
Obstacles

10 Letter
Dreadlocks
Evanescent

18

4 Letter

Ares
Arid
Arms
Atom
Best
Cony
Idol
Iran
Iron
Levy
Liar
List
Lone
Meme
Polo
Silo
Toga
Urea

5 Letter

Antra
Augur
Cubic
Dicer
Gears
Nerdy
Other
Rebel
Redes
Semis
State
Styes
Tales
Tesla

7 Letter

Agonist
Aroints
Avarice
Begorra
Bulimia
Caroled
Cerumen
Copying
Cure-all
Dirndls
Egotist
Émigrés
Epigone
Eremite
Evident
Habited
Lineman
Lunette
Mansard
Meander
Motives
Name day
Receive
Reneger
Repulse
Resists
Sesames
Synonym
Toreros
Urinate

9 Letter

Developer
Seaplanes

19

3 Letter
Dew
Ear
Ego
Elk
ENE
Ido
Inn
Ism
Its
Lob
Lot
Mil
Nod
Ran
Sod
The
URL
Ute

4 Letter
Doge
Dome
Door
Edit
Hope
Lest
Limo
Mere
Mule
Once
Seer
Shiv
Thai
Tosh
Wees
Yeti

5 Letter
Agile
Arise
Ascot
Assam
Dirts
Doest
Envoi
Extol
Mensa
Sugar
Trier
Vital

6 Letter
Gospel
Striae

7 Letter
Aerials
Ariosos
Episode
Googols
Herb tea
Lead-ins
Misuses
Nelsons
Ordures
Thereto
Trade-in
Venomed

9 Letter
Unreeling

11 Letter
Boxershorts
Erroneously
San Salvador
Welcome mats

13 Letter
Brothers-in-law
Solvay
process

20

3 Letter

And
Ani
CBS
Din
Dry
Ems
EST
Ice
Leo
Meg
Orb
Pub
USA
Use
Vet
Via

4 Letter

Arco
Base
Bops
Call
Eddy
Giro
Go to
Lama
NATO
Newt
Sups
Tree

6 Letter

Angora
Assume
Brewer
Karpov
Opines
Phobia
Repeat
Utmost

7 Letter

Acronym
Alumina
Artisan
Break up
Divisor
Emerald
Enabled
Glisten
Hideout
Ictuses
Inertia
Initial
Lamplit
Measure
Nairobi
Nostrum
Parvenu
Racemes
Rescind
See to it
Serener
Shrivel
Step-ins
Stomach
Succubi
Sunfish
Synchro
Vertigo

21

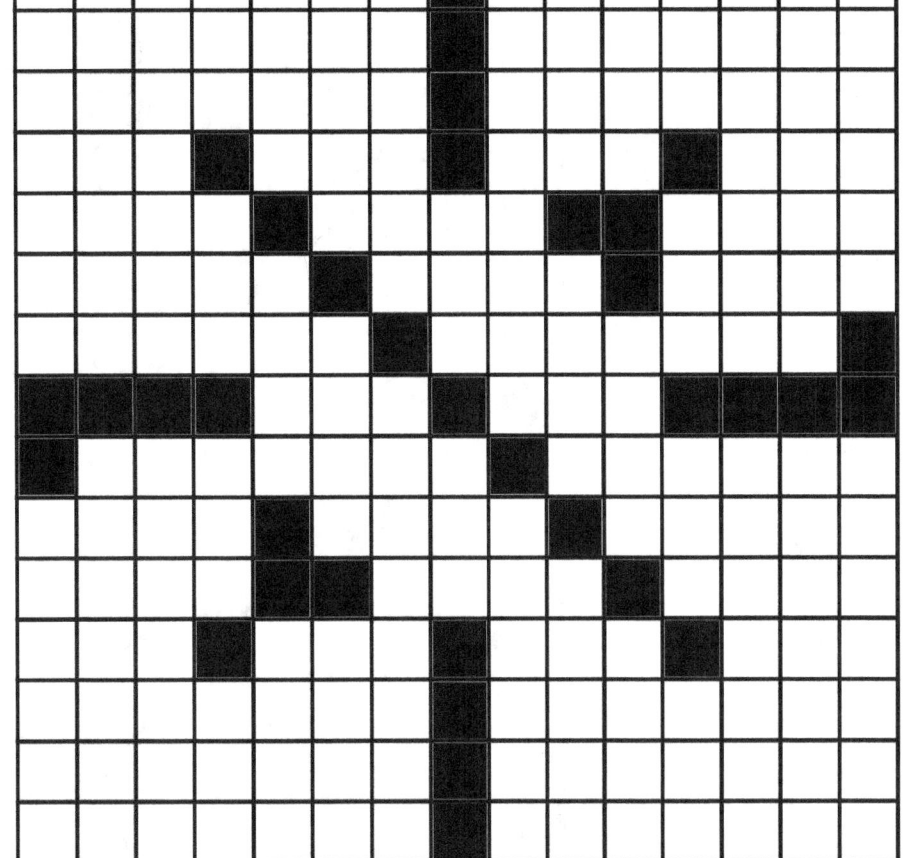

3 Letter
Ago
Ali
Ebb
Era
Flu
Gem
Get
Hat
Hoe
Mop
Net
Ode
Pal
Red
Reg
Res
Sim
Sly
Tom
Wad

4 Letter
Aria
Chez
Deli
Diss
Duos
Egis
Eire
Emit
Exit
Floc
Offs
Only
Otis
Reel
Retd
Riel
Said

Tale
Taps
Tiro

5 Letter
Devil
Lingo
Remit
Teach

6 Letter
Edemas
Enamel
Log off
Romcom
Stroma
Zigzag

7 Letter
Acreage
Ali Baba
Aligned
At a time
Croatia
Eelpout
Enraged
Ghosted
Labored
Matisse
Messiah
Mileage
Minorca
Oculist
Ontario
Overeat
Peatier

Seawall
So there
Steeple
Trading
Unheard
Wax bean
Zairean

8 Letter
Laureate
Swan song

22

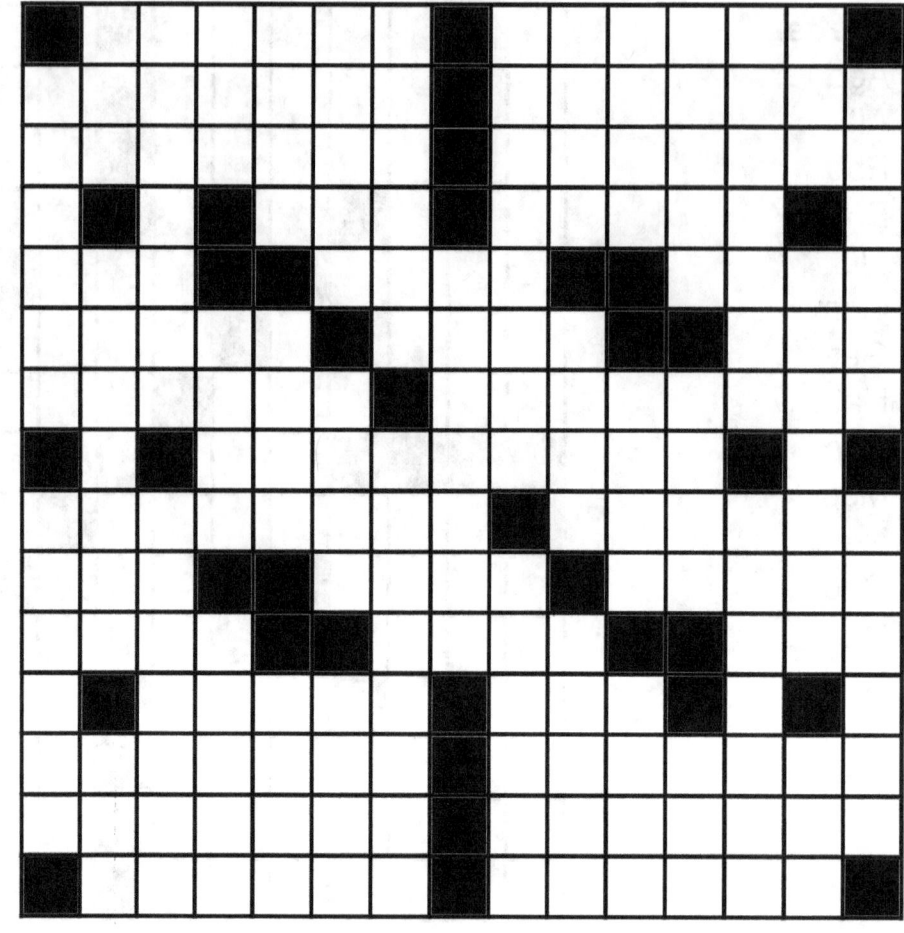

3 Letter
Age
Ale
Ate
Dab
Era
Ere
Gut
Hut
Lit
Men
Nab
The

4 Letter
Best
Desk
Edge
Grub
Lean
Lego
Lens
Ma'am
Math
Morn
Move
Naan
Prig
Rein
Tern
Tint
Toil
Wore

5 Letter
Arrow
Belch
Guilt
Ingot
Karat
Matte
Odium
Salsa

6 Letter
Alpaca
Change
Deduct
Endear
Esteem
Extent
Nugget
Rattle
Rector
Thence
Tittle
Tremor

7 Letter
Assuage
Austere
Basmati
Charade
Clarion
Customs
Elegiac
Fair sex
Ferrule
Glacial
Heretic
Rarebit
Reelect
Reserve
Titanic

8 Letter
Affinity
Debonair
Stage set
Violence

9 Letter
Graveyard

23

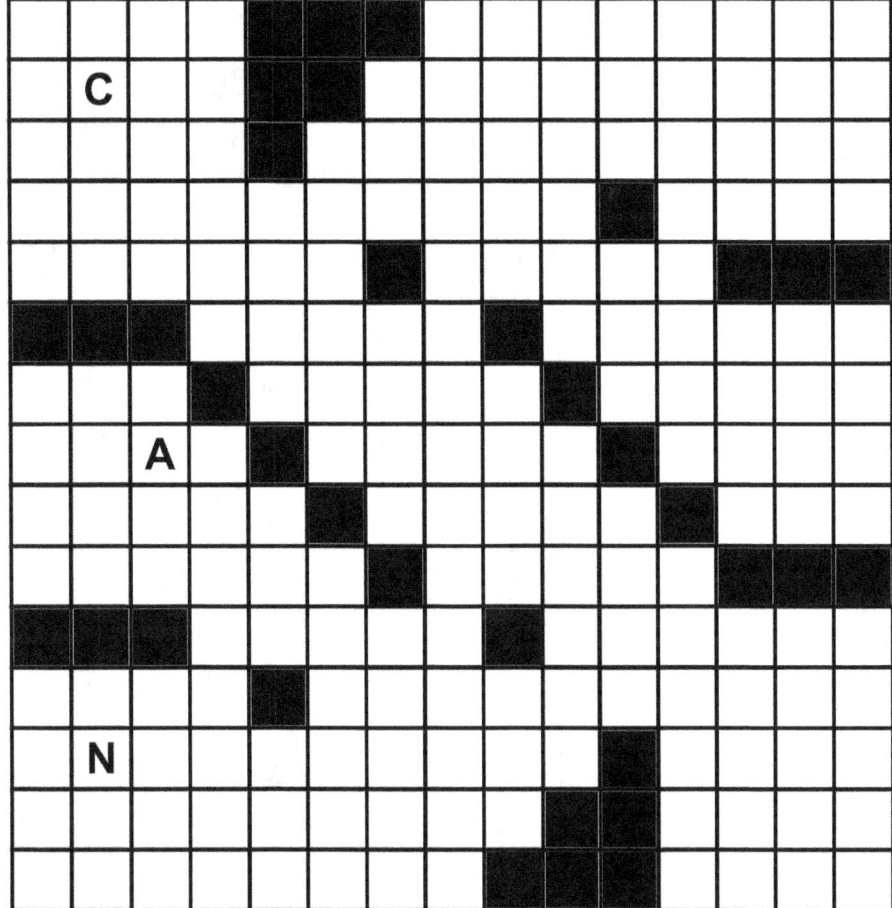

3 Letter
Act
BBC
CIA
Dog
Duo
Had
Mar
Res

4 Letter
Acid
Ados
Ages
Asea
Bozo
Brag
Burr
Cats
Dice
Dour
Esau
Guar
Inca
Laud
Mine
Mold
Narc
On it
Peas
Pent
Road
Rode
Same
Slid
Thro'
Utah

5 Letter
Acorn
Aztec
Cairn
Celeb
Diode
Dress
Durra
Egest
End on
Erase
Gnash
Milan
Needs
Pique
Recta
Samba
Snore

6 Letter
Anneal
Asleep
Cermet
Eddied
Entrap
Erases
Gossip
Pirate
Sendee
Toilet

8 Letter
Describe
Elapsing
Ethereal
Ischemia

9 Letter
Annealing
Ciabattas

10 Letter
Accordance
Brainstorm
Intimacies
Retreating

15 Letter
Inconsequential

24

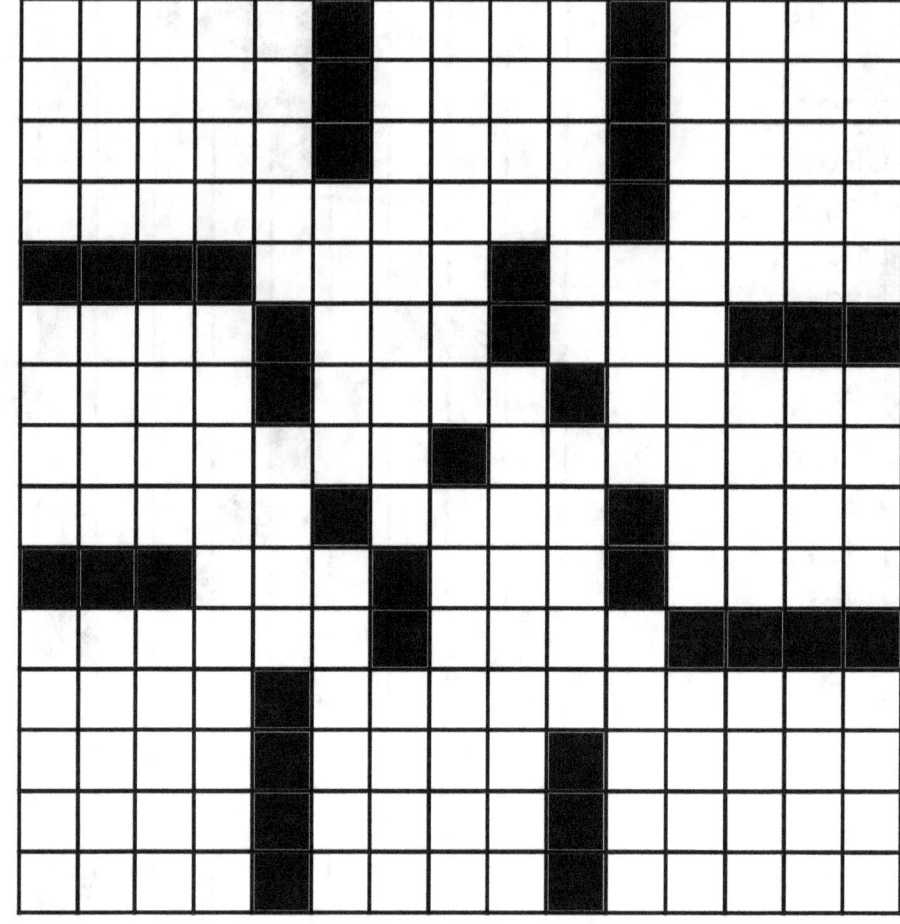

3 Letter
Ape
Lee
Pot
Via

4 Letter
Acme
Ages
Area
Aria
Arid
Aver
Bade
Burp
Call
Comb
Cove
Cram
Dang
Deli
Edge
Exit
Fist
Lean
Lees
Lira
Male
Menu
Miss
Olio
Omen
Oops
Open
Oval
Over
Pint
Pipe
Rest
Rite
Romp
Sang
Seer

Talc
Tosh
Vine
Went

5 Letter
Abaft
Alias
Arena
Clasp
Cress
Curio
Elude
Enemy
Lisle
Loser
Naval
Papaw
Peter
Pixie

Plaid
Pop-up
Rival
Unite

6 Letter
Access
Encamp
Escape
Mouser

7 Letter
Amalgam
Earring
Vanilla
Vestige

9 Letter
Botanical
Evaporate

10 Letter
Bridle path
Carry-overs
Commutator
Marginalia

25

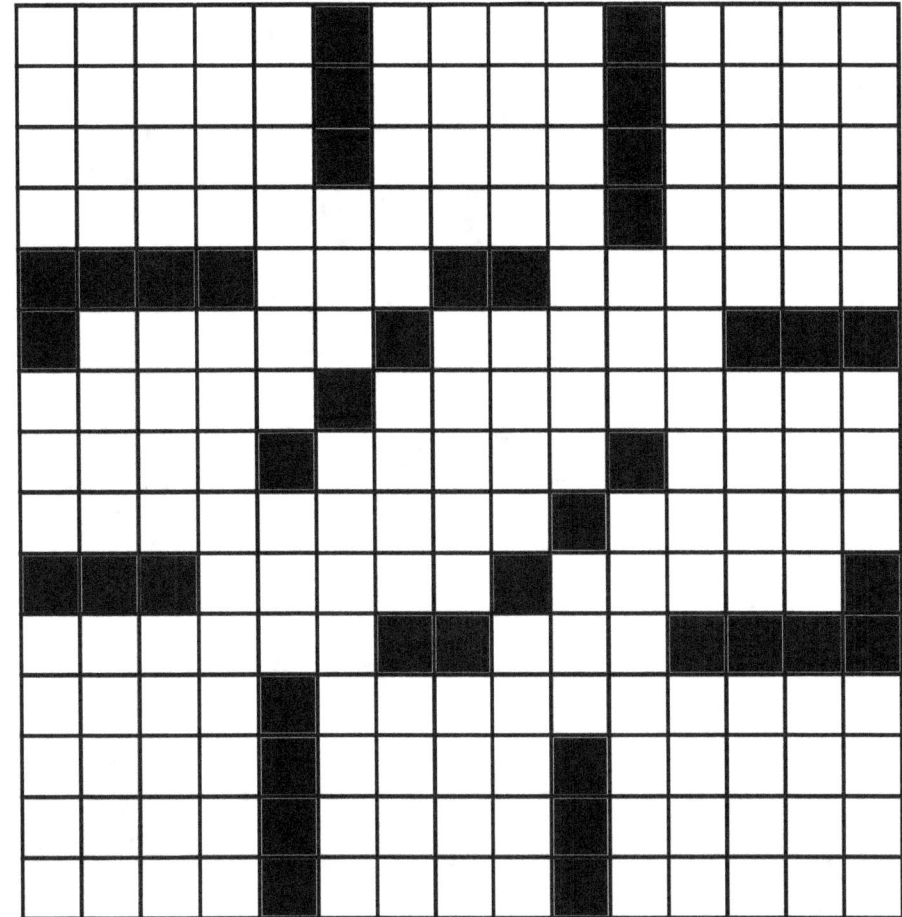

3 Letter
Arm
Ere
Lob
Orb
Ore
Run
Sac
Sun

4 Letter
Agar
Ague
Ante
Aria
Aura
Aver
Avow
Deer
Edge
Elan
Gaff
Go-go
Hard
Hero
Hole
Ides
Iris
Keen
Lair
Lava
Mare
Mire
No-go
Nude
Odor
Ogle
Onus
Peer
Plat

Rage
Robe
Swap
Vent
Wonk

5 Letter
Agent
Alarm
Alpha
Avian
Bread
Dower
Erode
Ferry
Gamma
Kebab
Laden

Overt
Paean
Pearl
Pleat
Revue
Rider
Siren
Snore
Suave
Testy
Trust

6 Letter
Apogee
Pointy

7 Letter
Anymore
Kindred

8 Letter
Blue book
Post-paid

9 Letter
Carnelian
Illiberal

10 Letter
Avant-garde
Behindhand
Free market
Privileged

26

3 Letter
Ads
Aga
Alp
E'er
Ego
Emu
Eta
Gad
Mad
Mag
Mas
Min
Pas
Psi
Ret
Ron
Shy
Sos
Tau
Tie

4 Letter
Ashy
Clog
Darn
Silo

6 Letter
Errant
Goosed
Lassie
Medico

7 Letter
Agnatic
Cassava
Cat's eye
Deadeye
Dispose
Egghead
Elegant
Eliding
Eremite
Harissa
Ideates
Impasto
Insofar
Métiers
Molière

Orients
Pachisi
Paupers
Preside
Pricker
Romania
Scarier
Slugged
Spheric
Sprouts
Stepdad
Take ten
Unseals

9 Letter
Editorial
Foreclose
Imageries
Tattooing

10 Letter
Betterment
Ergosterol
River basin
Trade names

27

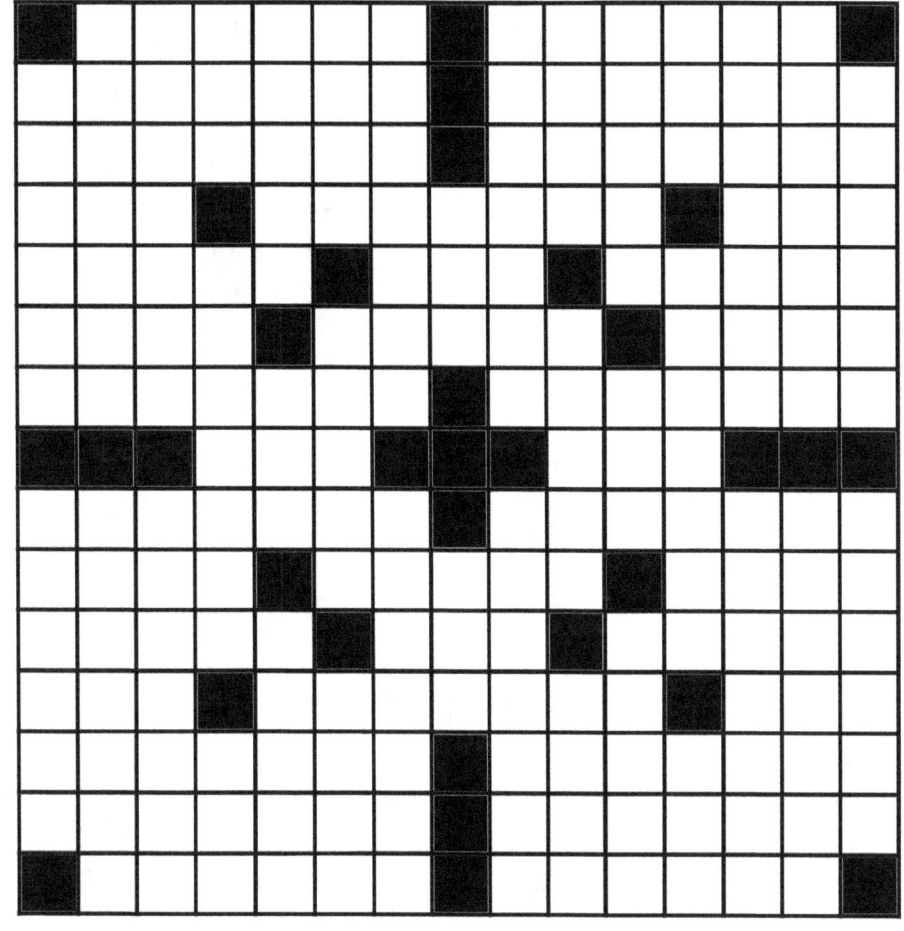

3 Letter
Bur
Cha
Gum
Inn
Ire
Lip
Lit
Pad
Par
Rev
Rim
Rip
Sal
Sis
Ten
Tot

4 Letter
Deli
Errs
Étui
Lean
Oral
Tied
True
Urea

5 Letter
Aback
Estop
Knaps
Redes
Rites
Scrub
Shrub
Smite
Ulnae
Umbra
Untie

Usury

6 Letter
Adagio
Elands
Nester
Repute
Sayers
Sepsis
Stapes
Tabula

7 Letter
A la mode
Actress
Anapest
Aral Sea
Arbiter
Atlases
Averted
Ecdysis
Electra
Eternal
Ferrets
Fruited
Garnets
Idyllic
Isolate
Nervous
Notelet

Oedipus
Ormolus
Rebuses
Rivulet
Rummage
Runoffs
Rush out
Stepmom
Threats
Titanic
Tritest

28

3 Letter

Ago
Ant
Ash
Bat
Boo
Eel
Ego
Eon
Ere
Ode
Red
Rig
Sex
Sip
Tee
Tit
Use
Van
Vat
Yes

4 Letter

Camp
Cart
Dash
Lard
Laze
Lobe
Memo
Mica
Neat
Oath
Oral
Para
Pate
RISC
Roam
Trod

5 Letter

Betel
Cruet
Dryad
Erect
Knead
Knoll
Livid
Oasis

6 Letter

Divert
Errant
Galore
Hee-haw
Ice cap
Repose
Teethe
Valise

7 Letter

Acrobat
Almoner
Armrest
Aviator
Azimuth
Caravan
En garde
Entrant
Eremite
Execute
Garrote
Gaseous
Haircut
Ice-cold
Mud bath
Paladin
Patriot
Serious

Vinegar
Wreathe

34

29

3 Letter
Ala
Are
Elm
Fop
Ira
Ism
Lye
Mat
Off
Res
Rip
RNA
Sex
Spy
Ump
Yes
You
Zip

4 Letter
Area
Lilt
NASA
Role
Roof
Skye

5 Letter
April
Aztec
Cocas
Laces
Lilac
Mommy
Muses
Seals

7 Letter
Abilene
Aliquot
Amasses
Annoyer
Arousal
Atriums
Boxings
Cascara
Ceramic
Curtain
Dadaist
Engorge
Foramen
Misdeed
Monocot
Oratrix
Ordeals
Ottoman
Pay dirt
Rampage
Redtail
Scented
Scoriae
Sea mile
Smartly
Streaky
Taxicab
Thrombi

9 Letter
Algebraic
Seborrhea

13 Letter
Filing cabinet
Nomenclatures

30

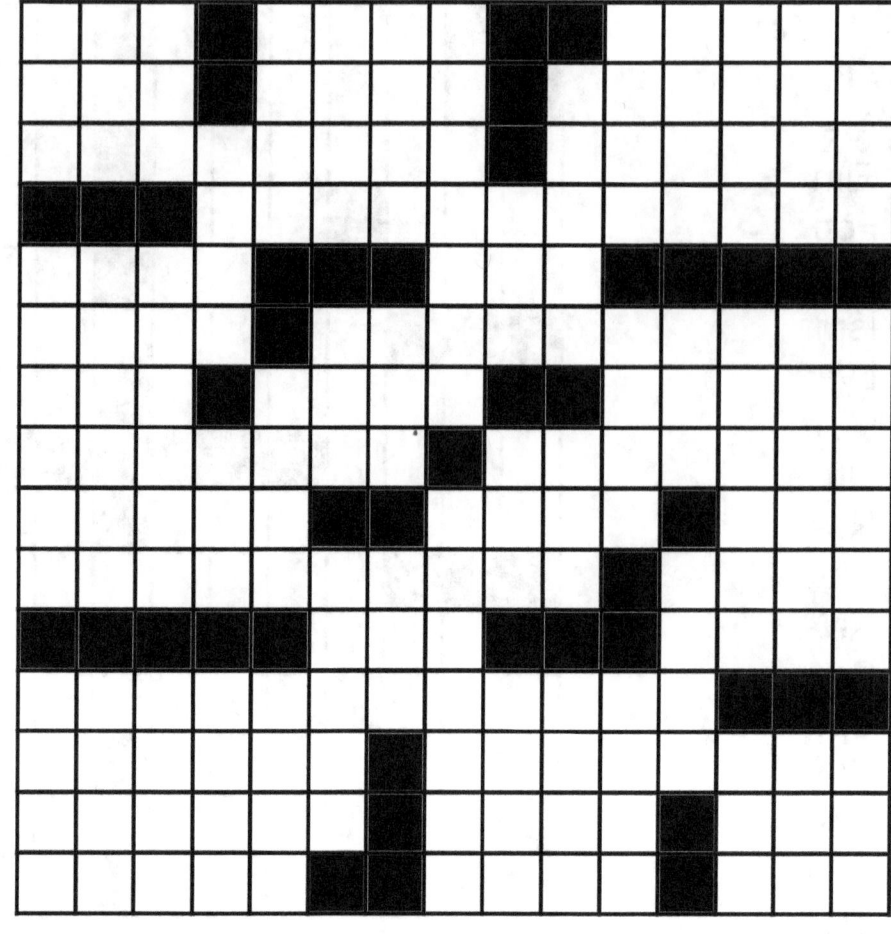

3 Letter

Aye
Con
Ear
Ego
Eke
Fay
Gas
Gin
Ice
Kid
Mat
Nan
Odd
Ret
Rex
Rip
Roe
Rub
Rye
Sex
Son
Tog

4 Letter

Acre
Aden
Army
Awry
Boom
Char
Edgy
Eire
Emir
Enid
Homo
Horn
Ilia
Ires
Lacy
Lest
Mana
Mann

Mete
Node
Noir
Only
Rode
She's
Sire
Sulk
Tees
USSR
Wish
Woos

5 Letter

Brims
Éclat
Ernst
Midst
Nubia
Ollas

6 Letter

Airers
Chorea
Iberis
Impala
Iodine
Moolah
Narrow
Natter
Oriole
Rarest

7 Letter

Enrages
Filbert
Lensmen
Roaming

8 Letter

Endanger
Monikers

10 Letter

Stentorian
Weather eye

12 Letter

Achilles' heel
Ways and means

31

3 Letter
Ago
Ani
Arc
Ate
E'er
ILO
Kit
Lav
Leu
Mil
Mrs
Neo-
Nom
Old
Ops
Phi
Try
Wee

4 Letter
Agar
Anne
Area
CERN
Dean
Dole
Dote
Drag
Edam
Egos
Ever
Fave
Hunt
Idea
Ions
Lade
Leer
Long
Naga
Near
Need
Nest
Ores
Oven
Over
Peso
Teed
Tsar
Upon
Ylem

5 Letter
Darer
Éclat
Incur
Items
Laden
Magma
Modem
Okapi
Penna
Piñon
Puree
Shale
Sting
Verso

6 Letter
Endear
Errand
Hetero
Marine
Outset
Overdo
Psalms
Roiled

7 Letter
Avenger
Endgame
Spin out
Yawning

11 Letter
Demonstrate
Dirty old man

12 Letter
Endangerment
Unscientific

32

3 Letter
Aha
Ant
Awn
Bar
Con
Emu
Era
Ice
Ire
Its
Lee
Leo
Leu
Nay
Ode
Ohm
Sot
Sty
Tel
Toe
Use
Yam
Yes

4 Letter
Amen
Anna
Anon
Ares
Axis
Bash
Been
Cent
Erst
Inca
Kris
Once
Pyre
Rain
Sari
Scab
Side
Stay
Tame
Thou
Type
UNIX
Unto
Were

5 Letter
Acari
A-list
Amity
Ankle
Gelid
Harem
Hicks
Manse
Nyala
Other
Slave
Slyly
Sneer
Wetly

6 Letter
Aments
Amnion
Apices
Bestie
Careen
Loaner
Scribe
Sweden

7 Letter
Antonym
Austere

8 Letter
Covenant
Staccato

10 Letter
Calumniate
Copenhagen
Nosy-parker
Spermaceti

13 Letter
Unceremonious

3 Letter
Duo
DVD
Ear
Edo
Ion
Lie
Sot
Tat

4 Letter
Also
Baby
Cite
Cram
Deli
Dreg
Gean
Guam
Gyre
Here
In on
Into
Menu
Ne'er
Norm
Oats
Olio
Ones
Road
Roes
Spec
Stab
Taft
Tide
Unto
Up to
Uric
Vain

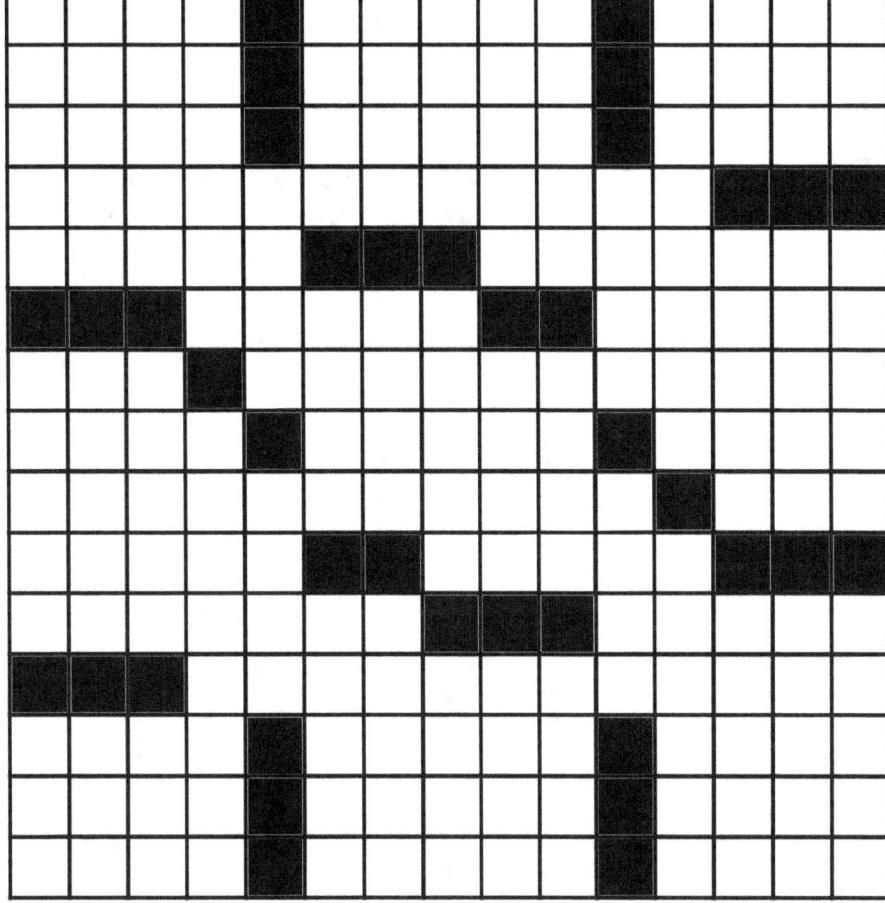

5 Letter
Admit
Altar
Amice
A-team
Attar
Berne
Boney
Costa
Elbow
Endow
Enter
Lenin
Octal
On ice
Oread
Otter
Radio

Rapid
Rhone
Set-to
Singe
Sloth
Snafu
Snort
Sodom
Testa
Tiara
Topee
Wests
Whore

6 Letter
Ounces
Slough

7 Letter
At a loss
Mealies

8 Letter
Cruelest
Scalping

11 Letter
Countryseat
Discommodes

12 Letter
Circumscribe
Polling booth

34

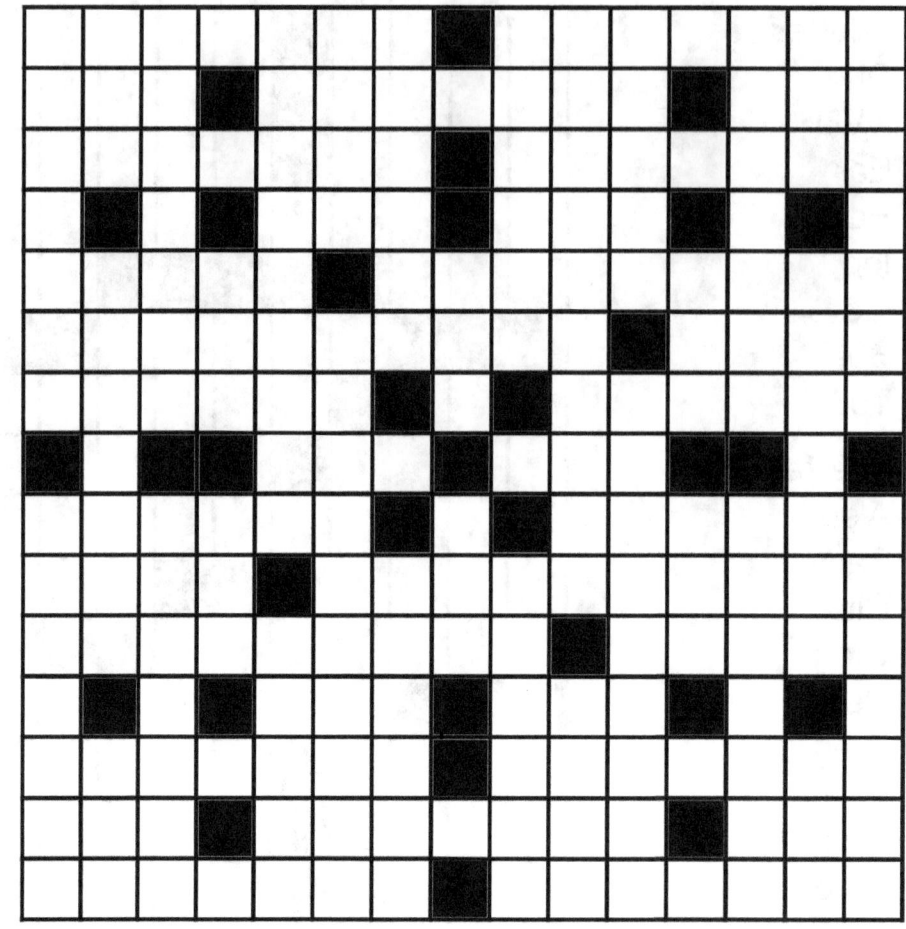

3 Letter
Ado
ANC
ATM
Bug
CID
E'er
Eta
Hod
Lei
Mar
OTT
Raw
Roe
Rum
Sou
Tai
Ten
Ton
USA
Use

4 Letter
Erne
On it
Root
Thru

5 Letter
Mania
Meeds
Rinse
Unite

6 Letter
Attica
Drapes
Evener
Incase
Nudges
Signal
Thresh
Viscid

7 Letter
Agonize
Asepsis
Estonia
Ignoble
Issuers
Navahos
Obscure
Oracles
Orifice
Phoebes
Pierces
Roister
Sadists
Scented
Smoking

Surname
Sutlers
Tracers
Tutting
Vomitus

9 Letter
Amidships
Asia Minor
Loiterers
Uttermost

10 Letter
Brahminism
Middle Ages
Occidental
Razorblade

35

3 Letter
Act
And
Ark
Elm
Ere
Err
Eve
Few
Key
Pol
Rid
Roe
Tad
Tea
Tot
Via

4 Letter
Ache
Apse
Area
Cava
Cone
Corn
Data
Deed
Else
Ewer
Held
Iron
Last
Mash
None
RISC
Sear
Sled
Spin
Tale
Tare

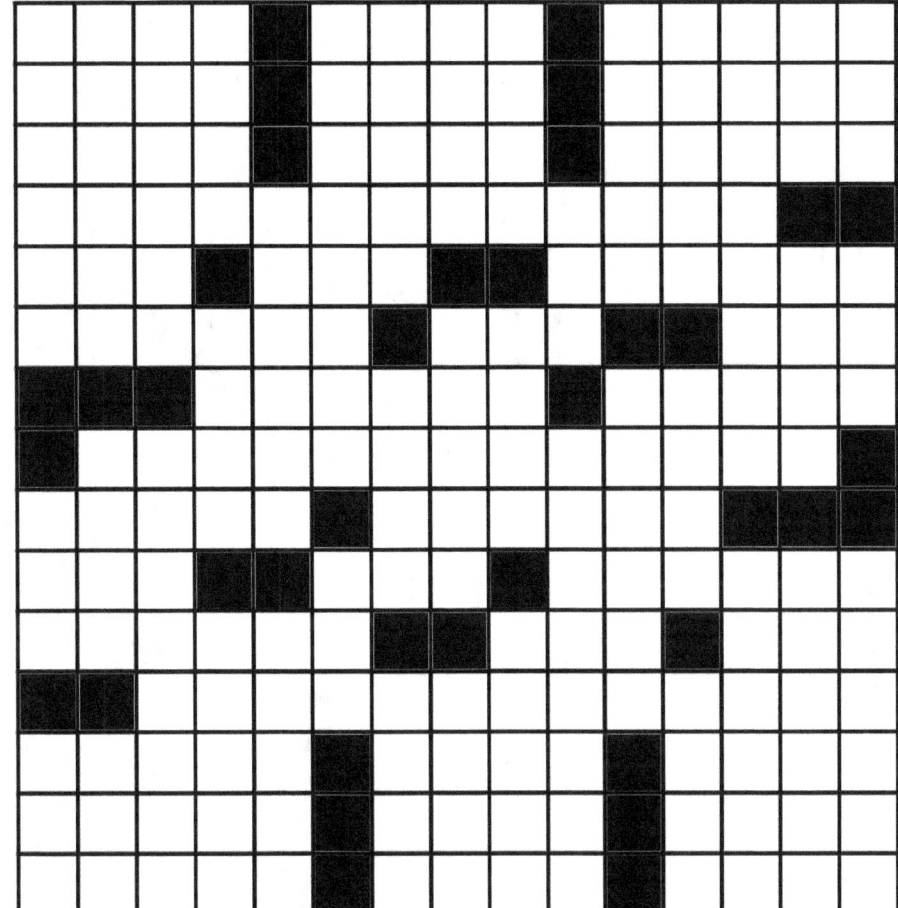

Tern
Ugli
Undo

5 Letter
Adapt
Allot
Award
Blear
Caste
Cubit
Enter
Evict
Facet
Fairy
Lithe
Macho
Mayor

Passé
Ulcer

6 Letter
Attack
Attend
Cravat
Facile
Genera
Ladies
Overdo
Rascal
Siesta
Speech
Steppe
Tonsil
Usurer
Warmer

8 Letter
Acerbity
Besotted
Detailed
Scenario

13 Letter
Bank statement
Canadian bacon
Reincarnation

36

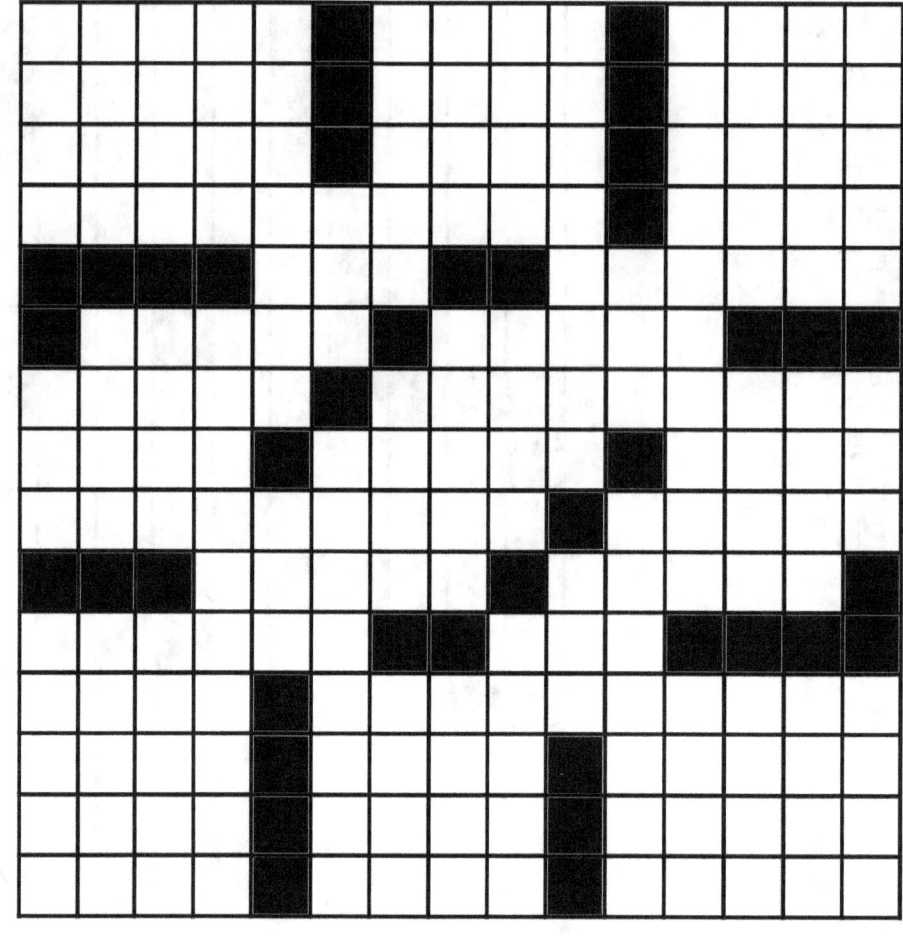

3 Letter
Ado
Dim
Etc
Ode
OTT
Pas
Sun
UFO

4 Letter
Airy
Anis
Anti
A-one
Aria
Arid
Atom
Cent
Eden
Flow
Glut
Guar
Guru
Hate
ICAO
Into
Jape
Kegs
Meal
Meld
Near
Onto
Oreo
Pale
Reno
Rest
RISC
Salt
Sets

Stoa
Twat
Urea
Uvea
Veto

5 Letter
Abort
Aping
Awned
Eagre
Éclat
Every
Franc
Haifa
Hogan
Latte
Nests

Opera
Plebe
Ranee
Risen
Roast
Sauté
Slain
Stave
Sumac
Telic
Toted

6 Letter
Rutted
Salami

7 Letter
Cyclone
Sporran

8 Letter
Comprise
Epsilons

9 Letter
Poison gas
Swordplay

10 Letter
Aberration
Lumberjack
Right angle
Saddle soap

37

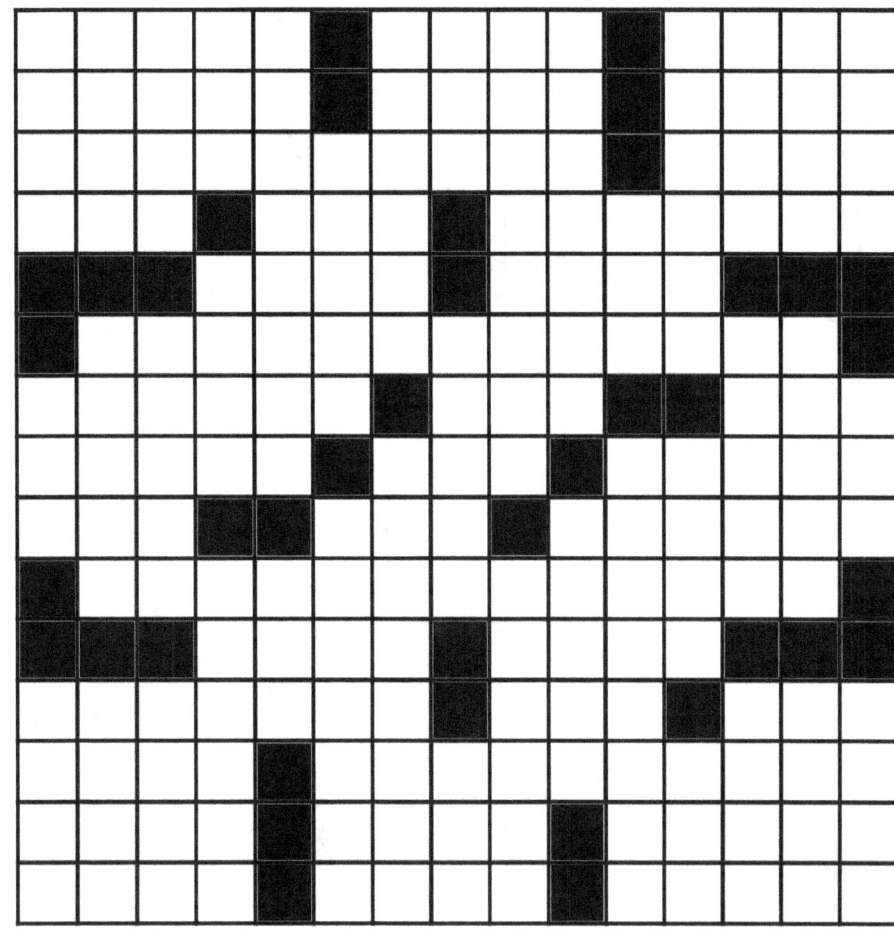

3 Letter
Bat
FDA
Gig
Hah
Hes
Ins
Lac
Lid
Nod
Nov
Oho
Ooh
Pin
Poe
Sae
Tax
Tor

4 Letter
Adar
Aide
Anew
D-day
Dole
Eddy
Egad
Emir
Ends
Idle
Isle
It'll
Knit
Lieu
Mere
Pill
Rand
Rear
Sago
Semi
Skid
Slam
Soda

This
Unto
Urns
Wren
Yous

5 Letter
Alarm
Aloes
Benne
Coley
Dylan
Epoxy
Error
On air
Raged
Showy
Sones
Sonic
Swung

6 Letter
Argosy
Byplay
Myrtle
Orgies
Sartre
Stiver

7 Letter
Assumed
Rupture
Supreme
Thumbed

8 Letter
Bringers
Diuretic
Grandpas
Loose end

10 Letter
Beforehand
Mendacious

13 Letter
Desperateness
Nymphomaniacs

38

3 Letter
ABC
Ado
Aga
Boo
Emu
Ere
EST
Ins
Moo
Net

4 Letter
Abet
Acai
Agar
Amir
Aver
Bale
Echo
Elan
Epic
Gang
Heat
Iamb
Iris
Isle
Lair
Male
Mire
Nero
Olio
Oreo
Pens
Pooh
Race
Saga
Saws
Scam
Sore
So-so
Tbsp
Thee

Toll
Ulna
Urge
Whir

5 Letter
Afire
Ameba
ASEAN
Auden
Boner
Cotta
Étude
Gee up
Gloam
Greed
Inept
Input
Ivied
Largo

Lasts
Nerve
Plume
Sieve
Tenet
Tepee
Trets

6 Letter
Apices
Glacis
Sahara
Sanded

7 Letter
Helical
Mahatma

8 Letter
Monsieur
Xeroxing

15 Letter
Collector's items
Duplex apartment
Self-examination

39

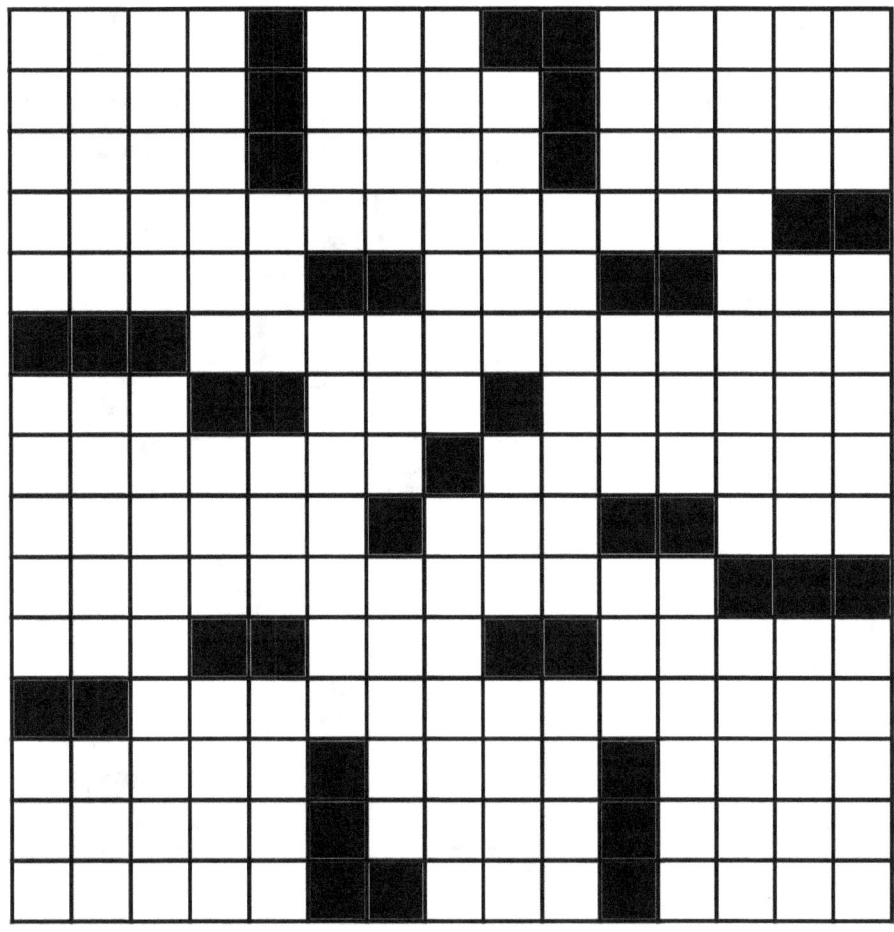

3 Letter
Ado
Ail
BLT
CIA
EEC
Ems
Ere
Eta
Etc
Keg
Lac
Leu
Men
Oat
OTT
Sin
Sot
Tar
Tie
Tot
Ups
Zag

4 Letter
Adit
Aloe
Amen
Avow
Fate
Ides
Item
Leys
Mace
Mete
More
Nags
Nine
Rail
Rant

Sews
Smew
Zinc

5 Letter
Aegis
Aerie
Flask
Guava
Incog
Items
Marcs
Occam
Omaha
Otter
Polio
Renal
Salad

Serin
Stale
Stews
Thane
These
Tying
Usual

6 Letter
Carats
Entrap
Platte
Yeoman

7 Letter
Academe
Chateau
Cuttles
Genetic
Leashed
Leg-pull

9 Letter
Aristotle
Tarantula

12 Letter
Anarchically
Polling booth

13 Letter
Characterless
Trade discount

40

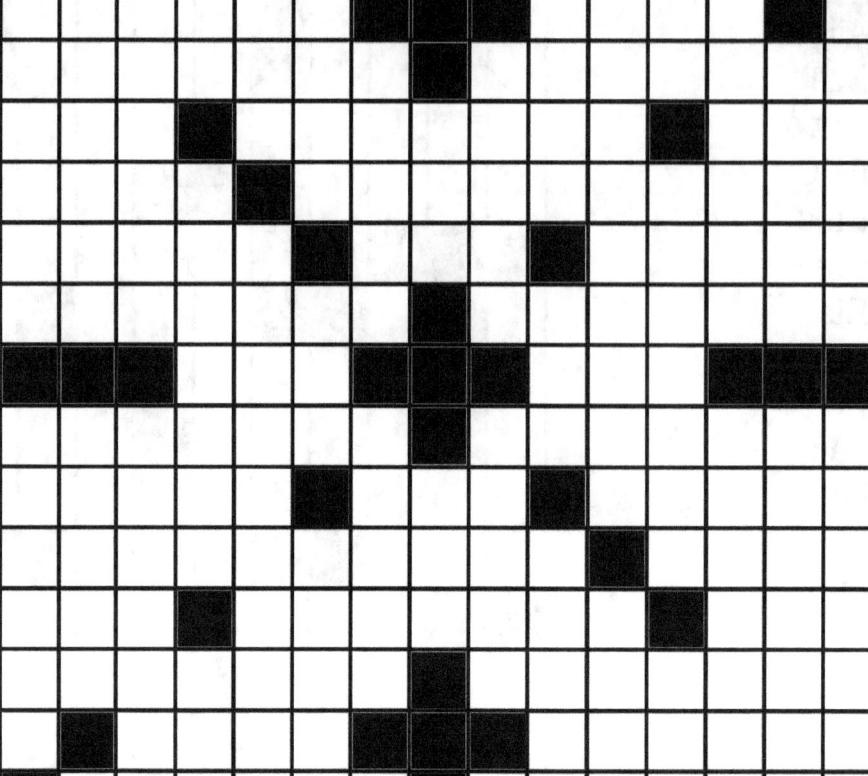

3 Letter
Aba
Aim
Aka
Ana
Ere
Him
III
Non
Oil
Opt
Rev
Sac
Sad
Sen
USA
Zap

4 Letter
Coke
Deva
Else
Sacs
Stub
Tsar

5 Letter
Amiss
Arise
Caned
Carol
Depth
E-mail
Endow
Korea
Oboes
Scent
Sepal
Suave
Tails
Yukon

6 Letter
Eschew
Oscars
Rachel
Tomato
Uganda
Vainer

7 Letter
Air mass
Amnesia
Benzene
Casters
Demagog
Elastin
Ellipse
Epergne
Harissa
Iron out
Lasagne
Poor law
Ravener
Reapply
Regains
Rondure
Slavers
Spassky
Streets
Swallow
Tainted
Termers

10 Letter
Adaptation
Caretakers
Come across
Slip stitch

41

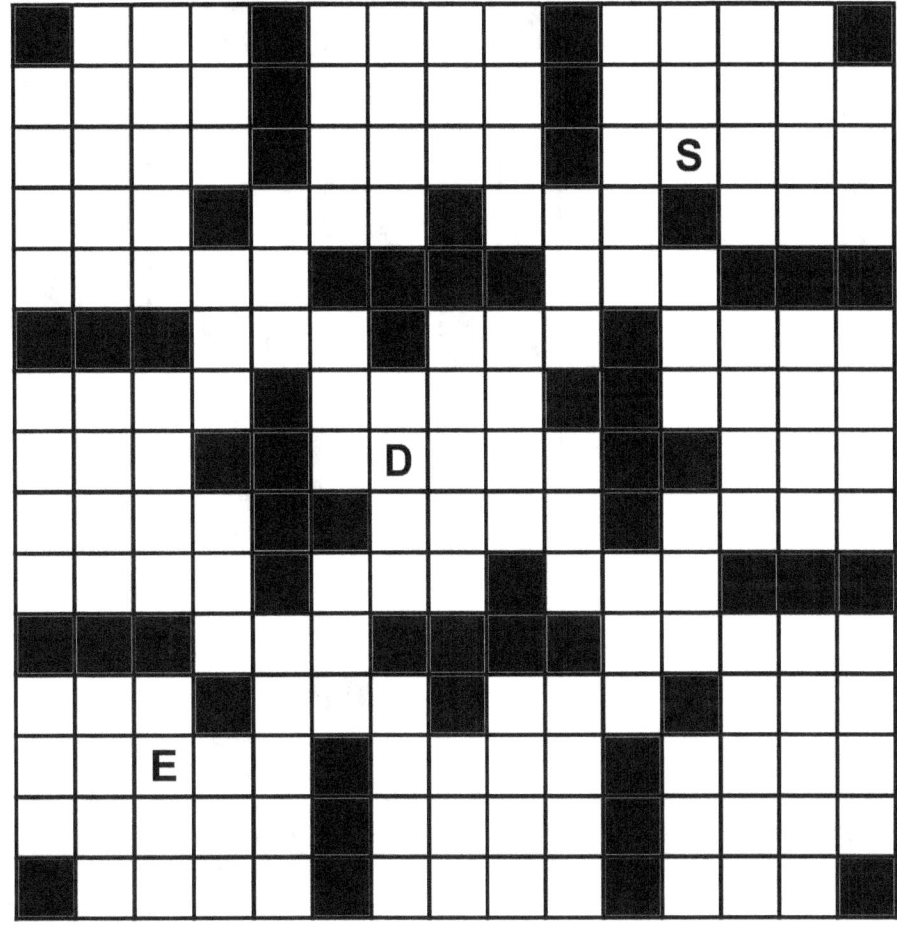

3 Letter
Ace
Add
Age
Ail
All
Auk
Aye
Bar
Bed
Cos
Dis
DIY
Era
Err
Fad
Flu
Has
Kid
Lac
Nun
Ode
One
Pea
Pun
Pyx
Ray
Roe
Rue
Say
See
Sty
Thy
UFO
Urn
USA
You

4 Letter
Afar
Ails
Arms
Axle
Band
Chat
Data
Ease
Echo
Eddo
Eddy
Ergo
Evil
Ewer
Ibex
Ibis
Ills
Nave
Noel

Oboe
Omit
Pact
Peso
Plea
Ream
Reds
Ring
Rosa
Saki
Sang
Seas
Seem
Ship
Sikh
Tape
Term
To-do
Tosh
User

Yeti

5 Letter
Ad-lib
Adman
Bowel
Debit
Ennui
Halls
I-beam
Ideal
Islet
Loren
Oomph
Relax
Shirr
Sit up

42

3 Letter
And
Any
App
Asp
Ate
Cru
Cur
Die
Dos
Ego
Eke
Eld
Eta
Gem
GSA
How
Imp
Its
Men
Oat
One
Own
Rat
Red
Rid
Too
Tow
Zap

4 Letter
Abet
Afro
Agar
Alto
Anoa
Deli
Demo
Ecru
Eddy
Edge
Eras
Gala
Hula
Lynx
Meet
Nice
Omit
Onyx
Opah
Oven
Pleb
Pure
Same
Self
Slab
Sled
Soli
Undo

5 Letter
Coati
Genoa
Grunt
Lille
Outdo
Owens
Preen
Prier
Sleds
Sneak
Sutra
Tetra
Tokyo
Ulnae

6 Letter
Ahorse
Azalea
Bestir
Carhop
Demand
Senile
Swords
Voodoo

9 Letter
Attempted
Delete key
Landowner
Ruthenium

43

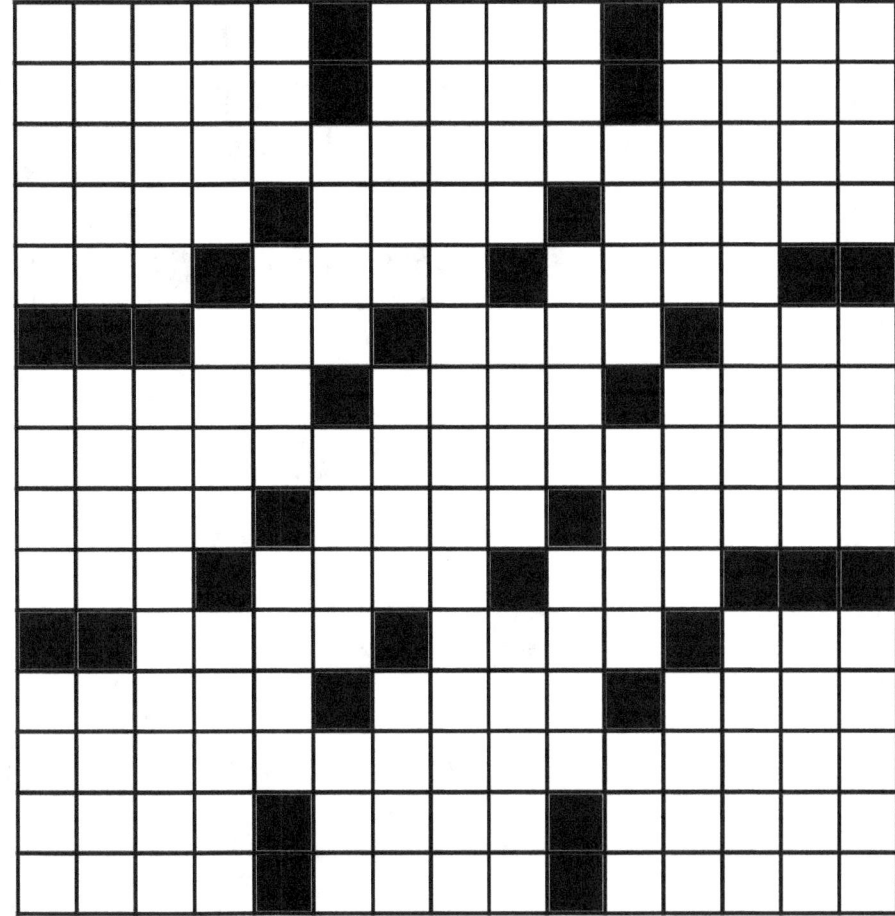

3 Letter
Ash
BBC
DDT
ESP
Ray
Sly
Sty
Tag
Tel
Wen

4 Letter
Adam
Aide
Amen
Apse
Bias
Blip
Blur
Buts
Clad
Cram
Eats
Eddo
Elan
Erst
Étui
Exam
Gate
Hear
Here
Leis
Leys
Lime
Mali
Marc
Mays
Mira
Op-ed
Open
Pane
Pupa
Rate
Rune
Sash
Sign
Sinh
Slag
Snag
Taka
Tarn
Taut
Trap
Tuna
Ulna
Used
User
Wadi

5 Letter
Apian
Avail
Bassi
Beaut
Beryl
Cress
Dagga
Duels
Germy
Laces
Ledge
Ocher
Pesos
Truss
Umiak
Uveas
Xylan
Yetis

9 Letter
Itsy-bitsy
Utilities

15 Letter
Dutch elm
disease
Earth-shattering
Plainclothesman
Situation
comedy

44

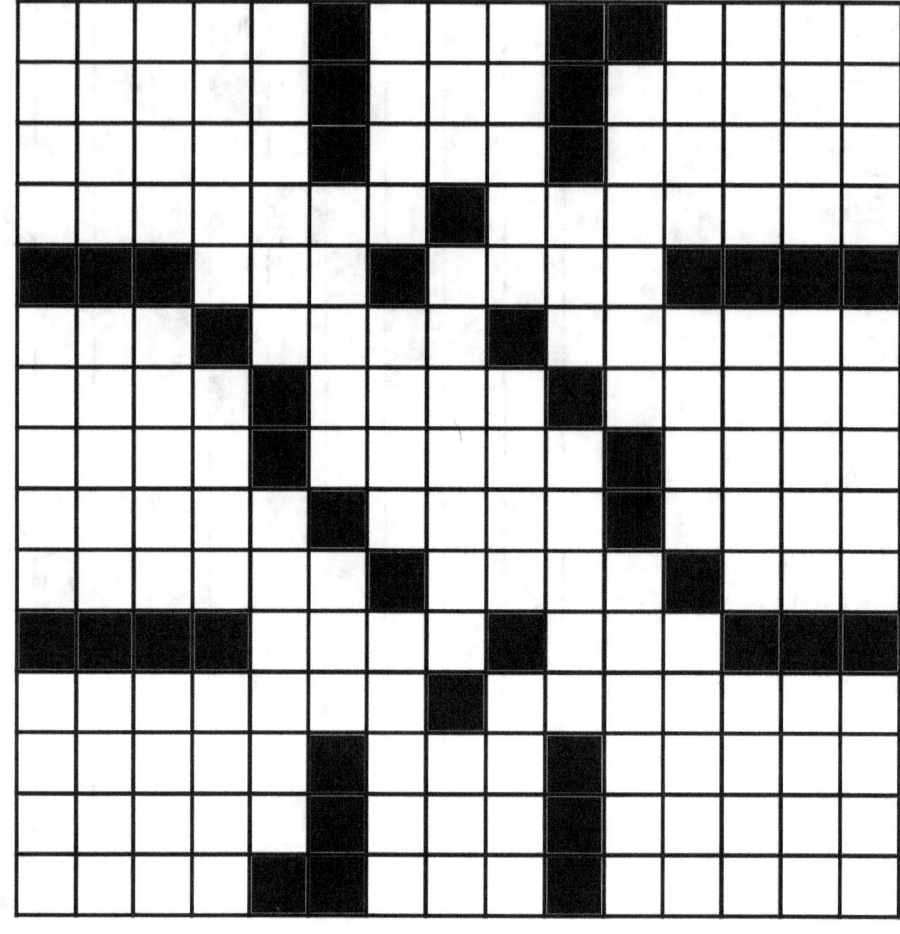

3 Letter
Ash
Ask
Bib
Bur
Cur
Elm
Err
Eye
Ice
Ike
Pal
Sac
Saw
Thy

4 Letter
Ache
Alms
Amen
Arab
Atom
Auto
Bale
Bloc
Boob
Dais
Dido
Ears
Edit
Egad
Grin
Ibex
Ibid
Ills
Lass
Lead
Lieu
Lobo
Need
None
Odds
Over

Parr
Pleb
Ruin
Sacs
Sear
Thro'

5 Letter
Areal
Arhat
Aroma
Blast
Diary
Dried
Éclat
Eerie
Error
Ewers
Gassy
Gulch

Havoc
I-beam
Larva
Lotte
Masai
Nines
Oboes
Paths
Saiga
Steed
Steps
Teens
Vacua

6 Letter
Bad egg
Clammy
Sat-nav
Stable
Teslas
Tyrant

7 Letter
Adrenal
Complex
Dilemma
Grieves
Obtrude

45

3 Letter
Alb
Ani
CBS
Cub
Dam
Deb
Goo
Han
It'd
Nag
Ned
NIH
Nil
Off
Opt
Our
Pus
REM
Rev
Sap
Spa
Tai
Tea
Tis
TNT
Top
USA
Via

4 Letter
Ante
Apse
Berg
Chef
Enid
Erin
Erne
Even
Fife
Fino
Foal
Hopi
Into
Lyra
Melt
Peer
Peri
Polo
Putt
Rove
Ruhr
Saki
Step
Tent
Thou
Tiff
Ugli
Uric

5 Letter
Aryan
Avail
Baric
Beret
Bravo
Dorsa
Ended
Ernst
Inane
Mimeo
Porto
Renin
Snafu
Steno

6 Letter
Caruso
In situ
Karsts
Ornery
Palace
Phenol
Runoff
Uproar

9 Letter
Eradicate
Himalayan
Ordainers
Unnatural

46

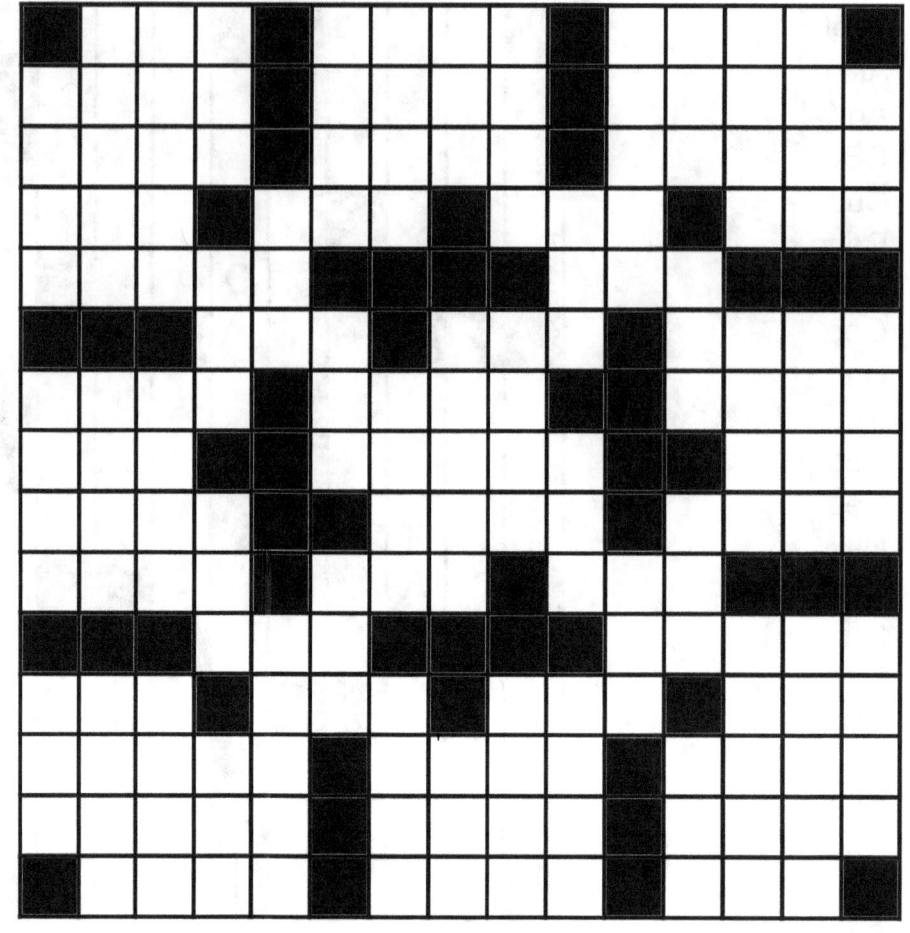

3 Letter

Add
Ado
Age
Ate
Ave
Awe
Boa
Bop
DDT
Dom
Ere
Gut
Ilk
Ion
Kay
Lad
Lea
Lie
Mad
Moa
Nub
Obi
One
Ono
Opt
Ova
Pas
Poi
Pyx
See
Ski
Tug
USA
Yaw
Yes
Yew

4 Letter

Anoa
Asks
Avow
Baba
Berg
Boor
Cede
Coda
Dhal
Dreg
Egis
Gaur
Goer
Go-go
Gory
Grok
Hi-fi
Hook
Iris

Kiwi
Kola
Lory
Near
Odor
Okay
Okra
Once
Onto
Opah
Owed
Pied
Reef
Reps
RISC
Role
Taco
Tact
Thru
Tito

Urge

5 Letter

Alien
Alpha
Canoe
Circa
Ebony
Gecko
Inbox
Input
Korea
Metro
Oriel
Set in
Toady
Valor

47

3 Letter
Ana
Ash
Con
Hrs
Lob
Mil
Mud
Pot

4 Letter
Bang
Bong
Doty
Et al
Iowa
Isms
Jowl
Juno
Knee
Kook
Leon
Loon
Maim
More
Omen
Rich
ROTC
Seam
Shed
Shmo
Spas
Stay
Tune
Vise
Wily
Wool

5 Letter
Adieu
Beige
Namer
Oh boy
Upend
Viral

6 Letter
Bracer
Denier
Idlers
Macula
Mimics
Oriels
Picaro
Talked

7 Letter
Aphonia
Asiatic
Brigand
Bush tit
Cembali
Cuckold
Enemies
Essayer
Hotlink
Humidor
Muslims
Overeat
Pimento
Stomach
Teenage
Tersely

9 Letter
Coercions
Purgative

10 Letter
Antibodies
Inamoratas
Militarism
Poorhouses
Sailcloths
Schoolmate

48

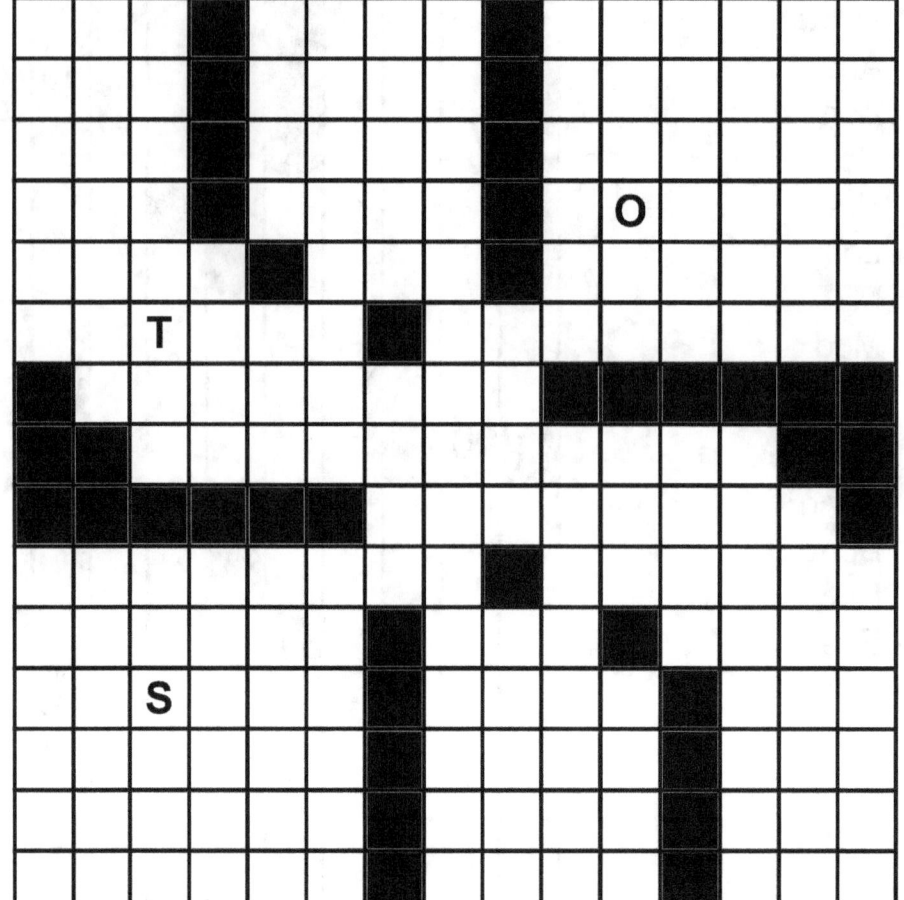

3 Letter
Arp
Boa
DDT
Hue
Ire
Lei
Lip
Oar
RAF
Sue
Tel
Yes

4 Letter
Asti
Else
Emit
Gael
Go to
Gulf
Idea
Isle
Item
Mate
Nuts
Oreo
Ouse
Ripe
Toga
Tsar

5 Letter
Lease
Usual

6 Letter
Abodes
Alpine
Elates
Eraser
Errors
Escudo
Estate
Idlers
Inhume
Loosed
Moaner
Needer
Nosher
Oriole
Pascal

Rattan
Repels
Satori
Seamer
Seller
Settee
Sorest
Teeter
Tittle
Totals
Tressy

7 Letter
Retiree
Road map

8 Letter
Amnesiac
Executor
Greenery
Octettes
Paganini
Partitas
Totality
Ursuline

11 Letter
Safe-deposit

15 Letter
Foreign
exchange

49

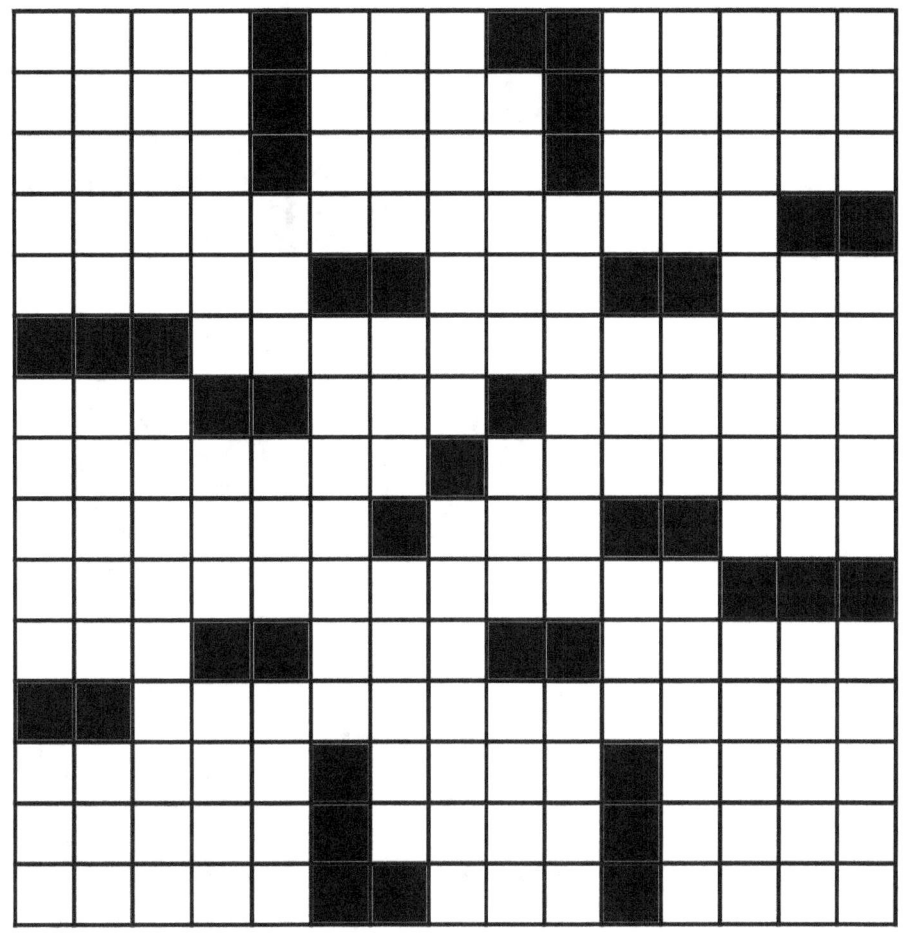

3 Letter
Ash
Bam
Cry
Cue
Eye
Gab
Get
Hem
Hie
Hoe
Ire
Leo
Ley
Orb
Our
Pic
Rug
Rye
Sal
Sty
Tau
Tie

4 Letter
Akin
Ales
Alto
Anon
BIOS
Blot
Dial
Dual
Elbe
Else
Erse
Fate
Geed
Gobi
Leon

Okra
Onto
Same

5 Letter
About
Aerie
Anima
Anode
Argue
Ashen
Chill
Deals
Essay
Idler
Metes
Modem
Outdo

Remit
Rinse
Set-to
Sloth
Spell
Ulnae
Yeses

6 Letter
Egoist
Enrage
Harems
Length

7 Letter
Broglie
Cumbria
Ongoing
Propane
Renters
Yoghurt

9 Letter
Loony bins
Ordainers

12 Letter
Herringbones
Luncheonette

13 Letter
Beast of burden
Laughing hyena

50

3 Letter
Age
Ate
Bun
Eve
Job
Née
Off
Pry
Sea
Tau
Tow
Ute

4 Letter
Acre
Anew
Cell
Hods
Ogle
Seen
Slit
Ugly

5 Letter
Agent
Amnio
Annoy
As yet
Catch
Error
Étuis
Latin
Refer
Riots
Russo-

Sat up

6 Letter
Arnica
Coffee
Elvish
Leader
Murmur
Onions
Pronto
Protea
Skopje
Skybox
Spokes
Steaks
Submit

Tenure
Trench
Xmases

7 Letter
Amasser
Carrell
Emeries
In utero
Issuing
Lioness
Malaria
Tremolo

8 Letter
Casework
End-to-end
Epidemic
Referral

11 Letter
Hotheadedly
Operculated
Tenterhooks
Teratogenic

51

3 Letter
Fob
Ira
Lea
May
Old
Sir
Ton
USA

4 Letter
A lot
Adar
Afar
Amah
Cyan
Drat
Egis
Emit
Gift
Hays
Hist
Ibis
Know
Lieu
Lily
Mile
Nero
Oboe
Open
Oslo
Otis
Rapt
Rule
Sets
Soft
Tact
Taro
Zigs

5 Letter
Amino
Among
Biome
Calla
Edify
Fit in
Fosse
Giros
Glide
Halma
Idiom
Incas
Ingot
In-law
Loath
Loupe
Nests

Niter
Other
Penne
Rests
Salvo
Scups
Semen
Snafu
Snoop
Tamil
Tetra
Tibia
Toile

6 Letter
Pizzas
Trying

7 Letter
Erelong
Whatsit

8 Letter
Et cetera
Spelt out

11 Letter
Shopkeepers
Subcontract

12 Letter
Movie theatre
Twilight zone

52

3 Letter
Age
CPA
Doe
Edo
E'er
Egg
Ens
Gap
Hoe
Ned
Old
Per
Rib
Who

4 Letter
Ados
Ages
Asks
Bier
Dana
Ergs
Etas
Feta
Idea
Idle
Item
Lego
Neap
Offs
Op-ed
Otto
Pity
Saps
Sari
Spry
Stir
Tole

5 Letter
Adage
Ahead
Arena
Borne
Civic
Creak
Eerie
Event
Giros
Hemps
Ideal
Iotas
Larch
Lepta
Naiad
Needy
Oiler
Phone
Sahib
Sapor
Sinai
Sisal
Sonar
Tango

6 Letter
Admire
Agings
Amnion
At home
Doable
Escrow

7 Letter
Alpacas
Carroty
Hairnet
Oarsman
Saintly
Stamina

10 Letter
Franchisee
Reembodied

11 Letter
Iron pyrites
Peripatetic

53

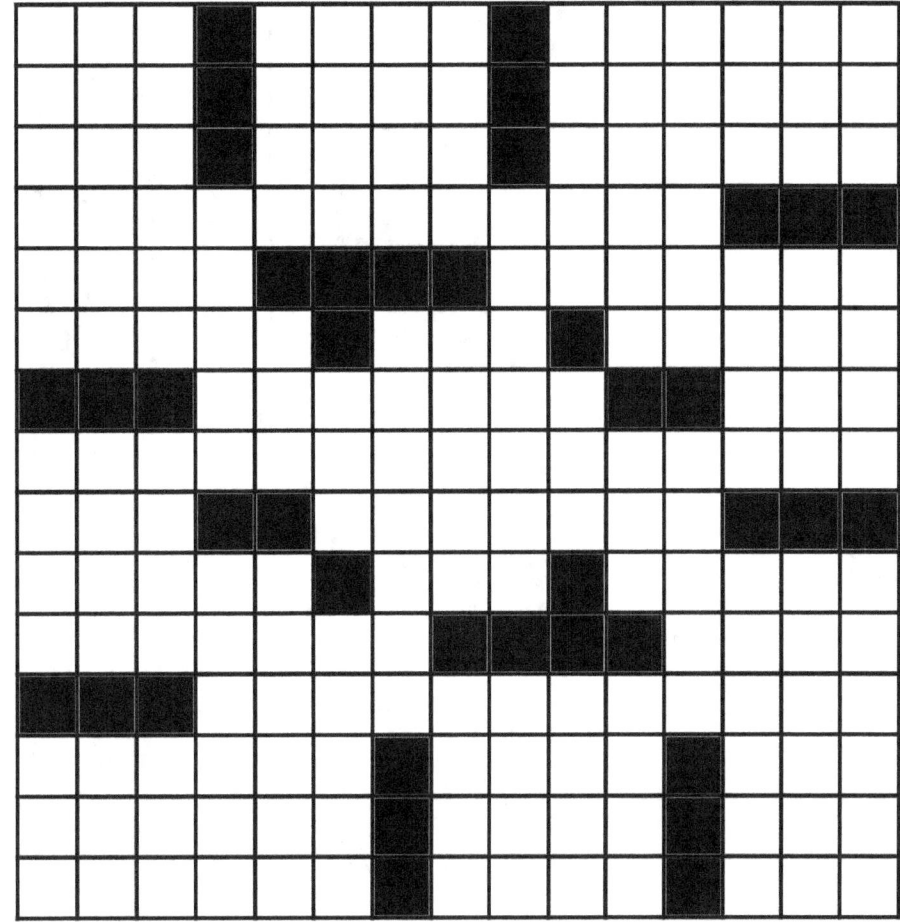

3 Letter
Ape
Ave
CGI
Chi
Ere
Far
Goa
GSA
Has
Not
Nth
Ore
OTT
Poe
Psi
Red
Rpm
Sir
Tic
Yip

4 Letter
Acai
Avid
Beer
Bosh
Edda
Gags
Ibis
Nova
Oboe
On it
OPEC
Oven
Port
Rend
RICO
Ring
Rive
Sari
Seta
Sore
Tsar
Vale

5 Letter
Aisle
Apian
Ester
Herod
Peeve
Ripen
Sells
Sitar
Tilde

6 Letter
Apiece
Desist
Ethene
Fatwas
Ignore
Impede
Instep
Old-hat
Pasted
Pryers
Rancho
Reared
Rectal
Ruiner
Spinel
Uganda

7 Letter
Chateau
Dialing
Emanate
Glamour
Guanine
Undergo

12 Letter
Hairpin bends
Wetting agent

15 Letter
Observation
post

54

3 Letter
Aha
Ale
Ali
Ant
Ash
Doe
Dye
ENE
Fat
Flu
Has
Icy
Ido
Ill
Led
Leg
Lei
Lot
Neo-
Ode
Old
Opt
Pan
See
Thy
Use

4 Letter
Baal
Emir
Gush
Holy
Moos
Oyer
Page
Pelt
Seat
Team
Tolu
Tref
Tutu
USSR

5 Letter
Adieu
Adopt
Haydn
Ladle
Liege
Noose
Offal
Peony
Situs
Strep
Suede
Surah
Tents
Unrip

6 Letter
Aspens
Driest
Duenna
Ennuis
Estrus
Fugues
Unsold
Yogurt

7 Letter
Antlion
Eyelash
Numeral
Orotund
Poulenc
Trinity

8 Letter
Landfall
Nuisance

9 Letter
Abradants
Flatulent
Lightning
School bus
Steamship

15 Letter
Platinum blondes

55

3 Letter
Add
Gel
Ill
Kid
Kit
Mat
Nod
Ode
One
Pig
Pip
Pit
Sat
Son
Ten
Wad

4 Letter
Abet
Agar
Barb
Boss
Brae
Camp
Cite
Debt
Deli
Edit
Egis
Espy
Euro
Ewer
Home
Iron
Lair
Lump
Oboe
Pear
Pity
Rare
Roar
Scam

Seal
Time
Tomb
Tone
Trey
Trip
Trow
Wail

5 Letter
Anent
Credo
Egg on
Feint
Grits
Motif
Oiled
Tenth

6 Letter
Assert
Cleric
Cradle
Dosage
Entice
Euchre
Goalie
Impair
Merely
Needle
Reefer
Throne

7 Letter
Crooner
Destiny
Ecology
Incline
Trustee
Twelfth

8 Letter
Deselect
Stroller

12 Letter
Below the belt
Electroplate

56

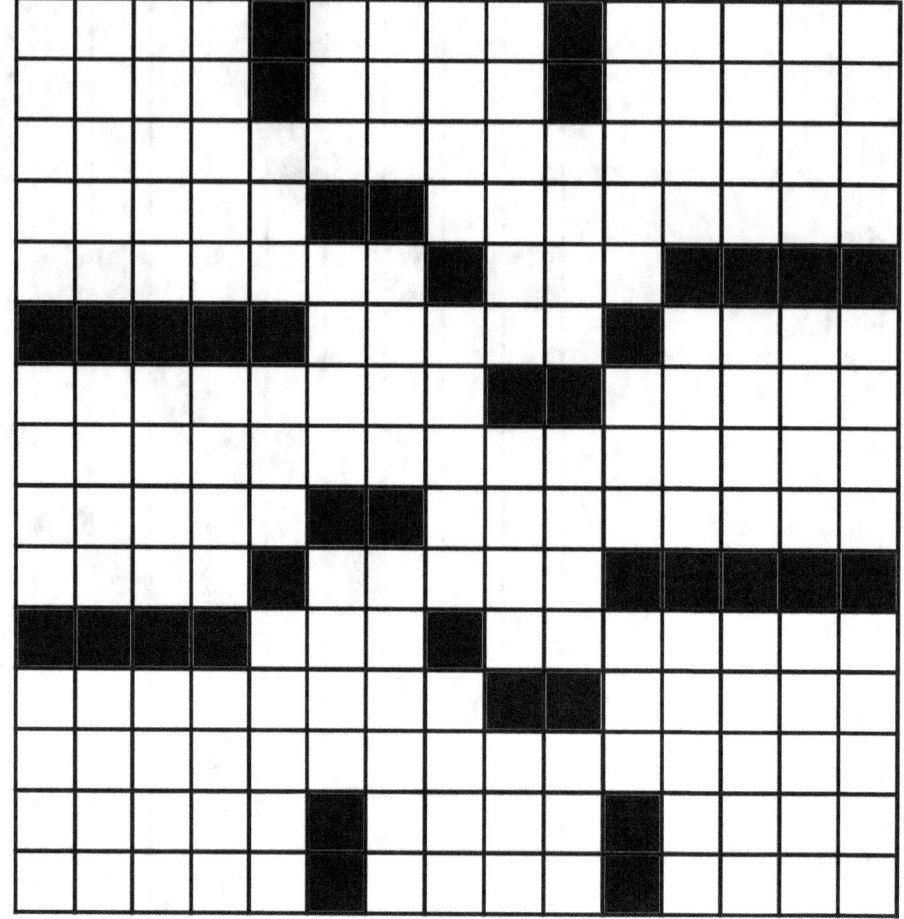

3 Letter
Arc
Dry
Eke
For
Gnu
Gum
Imp
Ore
Rya
Wit

4 Letter
Alit
Amen
Ammo
Arum
C'mon
Epic
Espy
Fays
Fork
Gigs
Hemp
Iron
Lade
Lots
Maps
Mole
Nipa
Owls
Peer
Penn
Pict
Pike
Riot
Rule
Ruse
She's
Sian
Soya
Stoa
Stye

Undo
Unit
Ursa
Yore

5 Letter
Allah
Amole
Arian
Ascot
Fichu
Folio
Genes
Gipsy
Hairy
Nones
Relit
Snafu
Snarl
Stale

Styes
Tease
Tilde
Timor
Untie
Veals
Yogic

6 Letter
Nullah
Steres

7 Letter
Cravats
Unclasp

8 Letter
Guerdons
Operetta
Sacredly
Sri Lanka

15 Letter
Cigarette papers
Immunologically
Insurance policy

57

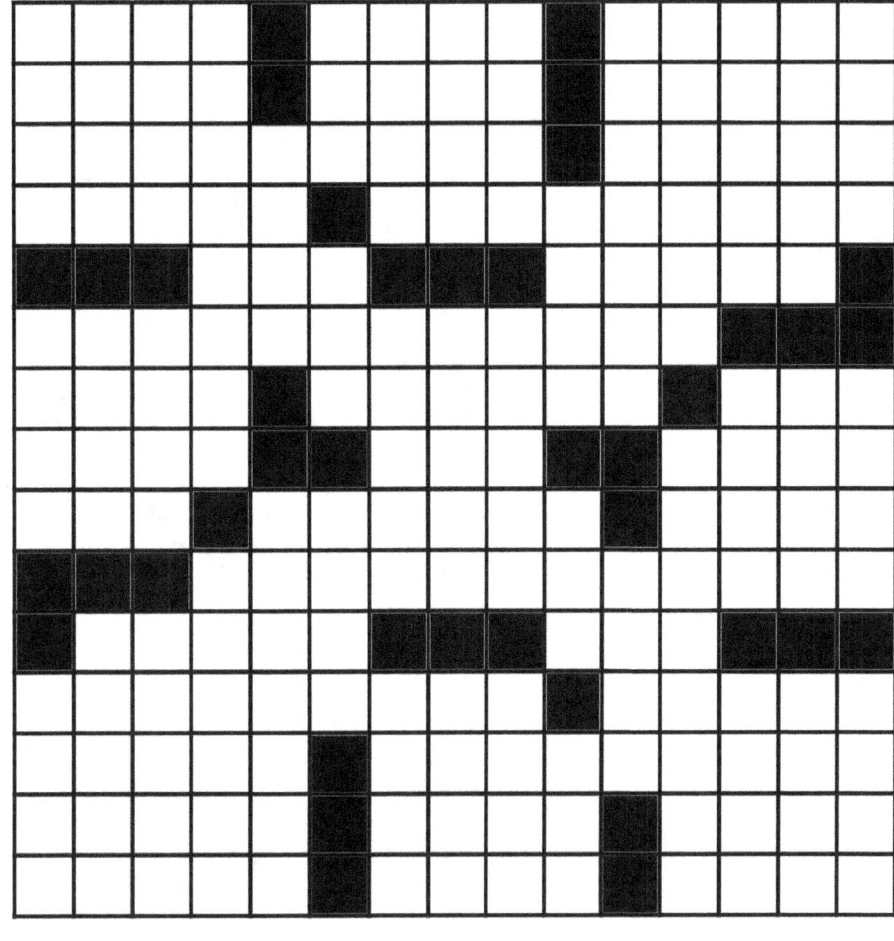

3 Letter
Arm
Eel
Inn
Mar
Ski
Spa
Tam
Tea
Ted

4 Letter
Amen
Area
Aril
Asia
Brad
Cagy
Char
Curb
Deny
Dreg
Earn
Echo
Eked
Erie
Esau
File
Haka
Hare
Hasp
Herb
Iffy
Lady
Lama
Menu
Oast
Open
Pure
Rick
Scam
Seep
Sill

Sods
Teem
Thai
Urea
Yell

5 Letter
Abide
Ailed
Cable
Cacao
Cocos
Comte
Demur
Glogg
Idaho
Image
Khats
Licks
Nicad

Olios
Pukka
Scram
Yeses

6 Letter
Idiocy
Nem con
Nougat
Smudge

7 Letter
Lincoln
Nutmegs

8 Letter
Backslap
Chemical

9 Letter
Bluecoats
Calumnies
Friedcake
Saccharin

12 Letter
Outlandishly
Supreme Being

58

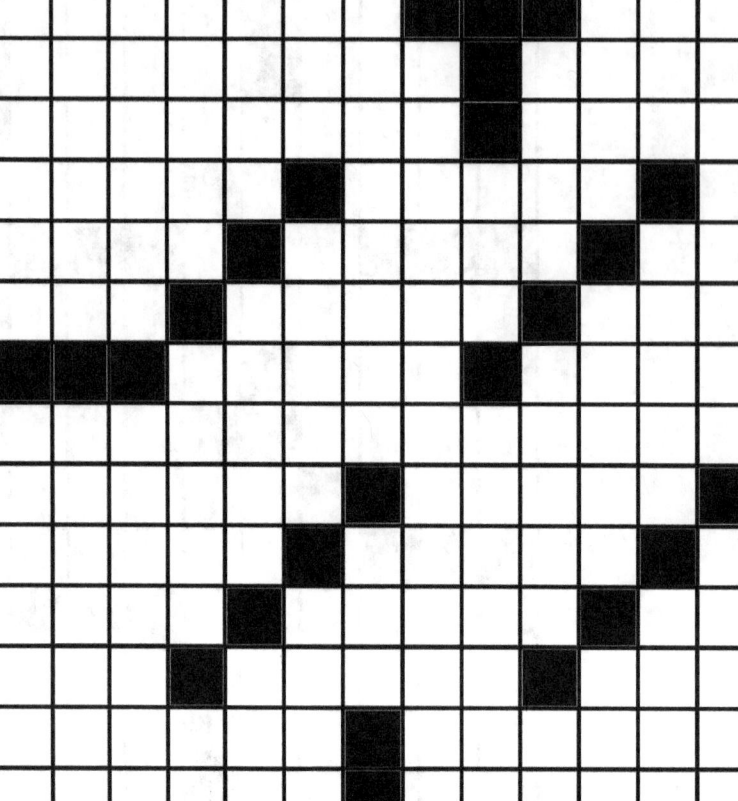

3 Letter
Amp
Bet
Elk
Hem
Hoe
Par
Pas
Sap
Tar
Wet

4 Letter
Bene
Carb
Deny
Goal
Mako
Rudd
Seer
Sods
Spur
Veal

5 Letter
Abbas
Bares
Duper
Ember
Erect
H-bomb
Hover
Levee
Libel
Malta
Rakes
Sassy
Scent
Scums
Shawm

Teens
Tenet
Terce
Tinct
Tolls
Umber
Veldt

6 Letter
Attest
Camber
Crimea
Entail
Errand
Goonie
Helios
Insole
Meanly

Odessa
Seeped
Tilers

7 Letter
Accused
Grossly

8 Letter
Answerer
Detainee
Discases
Meatless
On camera
Riparian
Snake oil
Timbuktu
Trampler
Tree ring

Usurpers
Wiseacre

13 Letter
Rubberneckers

15 Letter
Double
entendres

59

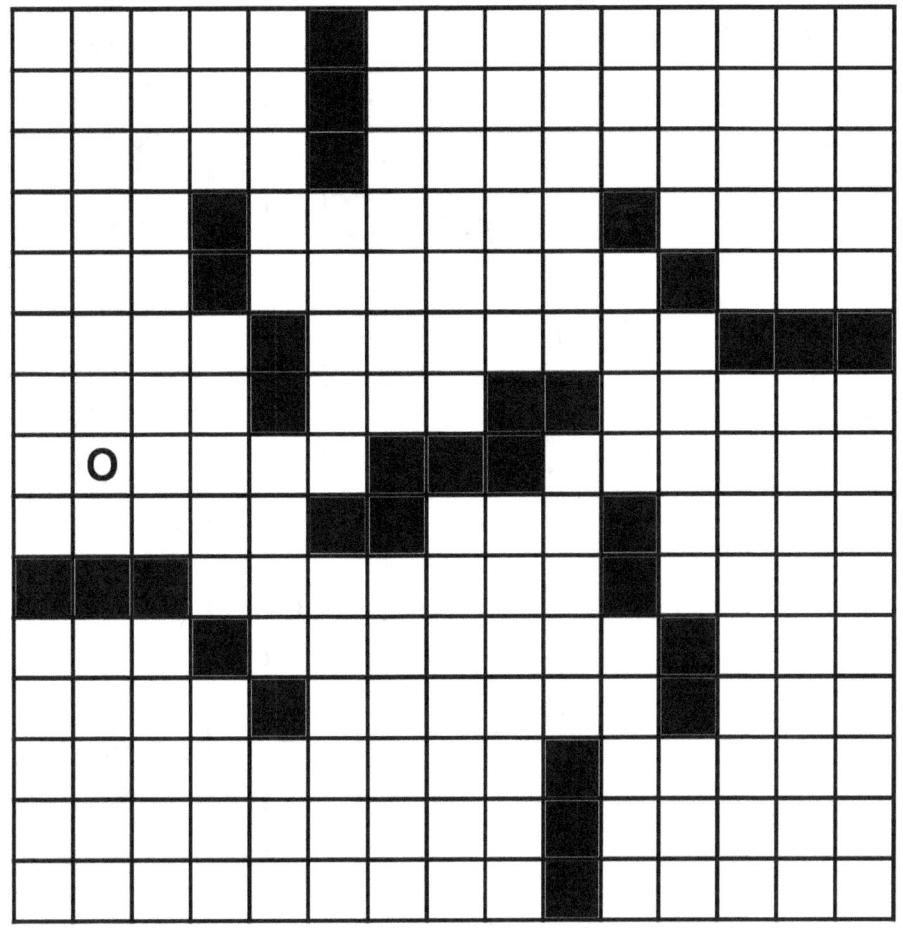

3 Letter
Ace
Ana
Arm
Ate
Baa
Bio
Ems
Ice
Kit
Men
NIH
Rot

4 Letter
Anoa
Area
Arum
Atom
Bier
Eyed
Lets
Line
Shay
Yeti

5 Letter
Argal
Calve
Ebbed
Emote
Erica
Essay
Euler
Inane
Kafir
Lille
Loess
Panel
Renin

Sales
Shell
Skill
Sonic
Tonne
Totem
Ukase

6 Letter
Attend
Bootie
Gasser
Longer
Piping
Smiley
Splash
Velvet

7 Letter
Aliases
Amalgam
Bullace
Dailies
Eugenia
Larders
Leg-pull
Louvers

9 Letter
Alabaster
Alienable
Automaton
Eyeshades
Fantasias
Innocence
Motor home

Nineteens
Oratorios
Re-emerges
Sentinels
Separable

60

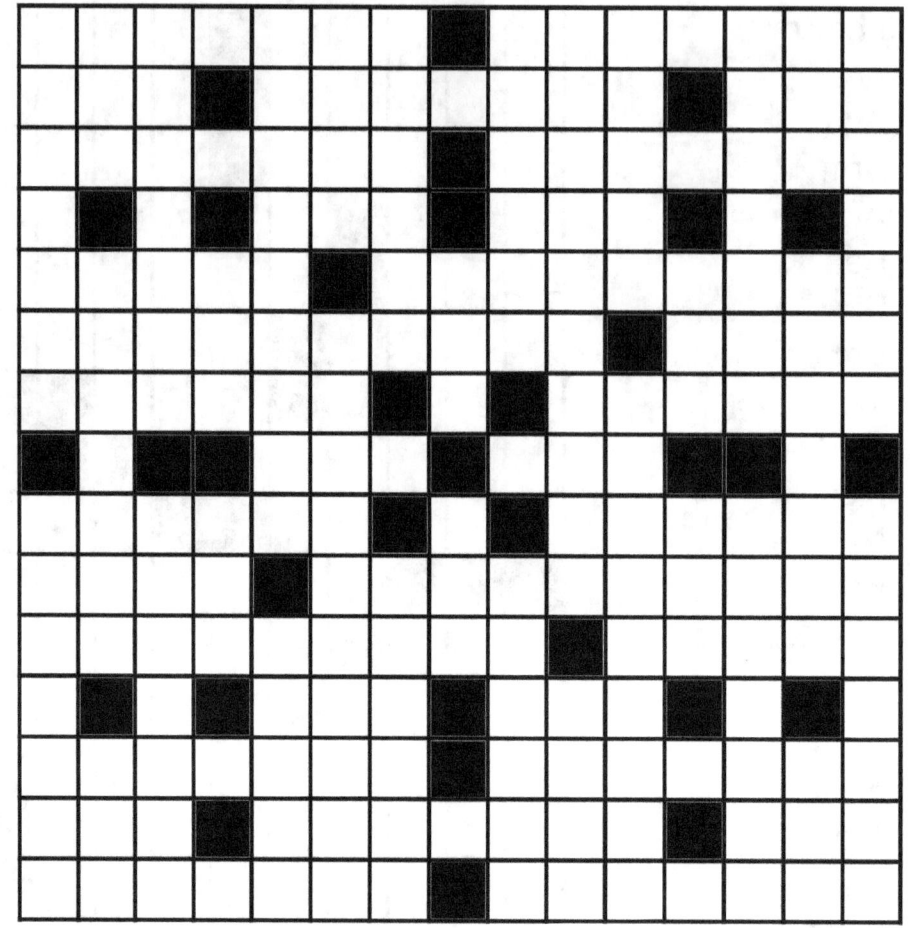

3 Letter
Aga
Ala
Ate
Awn
Bra
Cue
Deb
E'en
Ere
Err
Gat
Goo
Ins
Lid
Nut
Ops
OTT
Sat
Six
Soh

4 Letter
Guam
Idle
Pint
Wool

5 Letter
Harem
House
Incan
Tango

6 Letter
Aussie
Cabbie
Dear me
Eclair
Otiose
Sooner
Tangly
Vacate

7 Letter
Agonize
Asepsis
Binding
Carbarn
Densely
Eggcups
Egoists
Emerges
Ethical
Insight
Lolling
Necktie
Odonata
Oppress
Othello

Peat bog
Rubrics
Seismal
So there
V-shaped

9 Letter
Adaptable
Estimable
Pesthouse
Solenoids

10 Letter
Handspring
Statistics
Treehopper
Zealotries

61

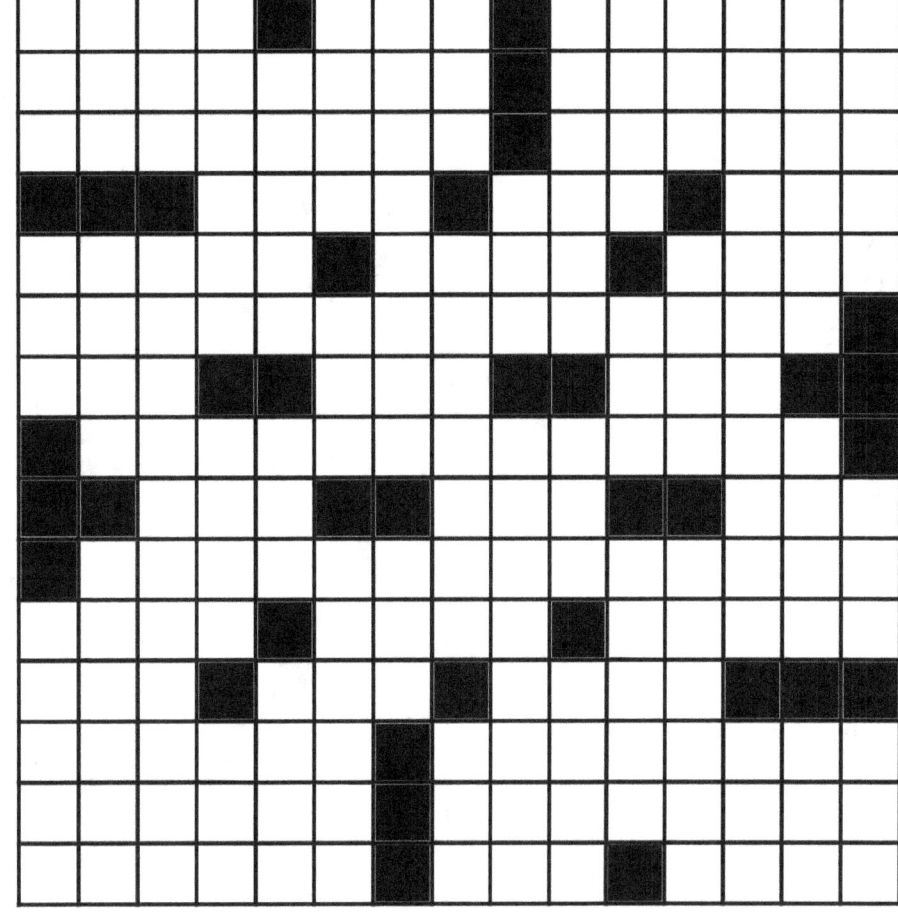

3 Letter
Add
Aha
Alp
Ant
Ape
ATM
Bee
Dub
Ens
EST
Ido
Imp
Lie
Met
Nag
Net
Nov
Oct
One
Pat
Pot
Rag
Rig
Rpm
Rye
She
Tie
Won
Yen
Yin

4 Letter
Able
Awes
Ayah
Dona
Emit
Fief
Flea
Haul
Idol
Less
Peer
Roof

Thee
Twit
Webs
Yegg

5 Letter
Arena
Howls
Imide
Irate
Mused
Payee

6 Letter
Aachen
Elands
Impair
Jerboa
Jinnee
Levied
Nimble
Oilier
Outcry
Sneers
Strath
Whiten

7 Letter
Bumbles

8 Letter
Einstein
Entrance
Hibernia
Postpone
Seed corn
Unchaste

11 Letter
Attributive
Babylonians

13 Letter
Fringe benefit

14 Letter
Above-mentioned
Mother superior

62

3 Letter
Ado
Ask
EEC
Hit
NIH
PTA
Tad
URL

4 Letter
Aria
Avon
Body
Dead
Enol
It'll
Maps
SETI
Sire
Tray
Typo
Vega

5 Letter
Arena
Aroma
Canis
Crone
Dosed
Fjord
Herbs
Ileus
Kline
Knock
Lends
Moils
Mynah
Omega
Slant

Snafu
Snail
Straw
Tacos
Tetra
Wyatt
Yogic

6 Letter
Animus
Fainer
Gdansk
Lienal
Racoon
Sluice
Stream
Theses
Tirade

Trendy

7 Letter
Armenia
Beanbag
Buttock
Dunnage
Gallant
Laddies
Sad sack
Sit back

8 Letter
Cesarean
Ferryman
Jalapeño
One-piece

9 Letter
Anathemas
Negritude
Reclaimed
Strip mall
Trattoria
Treatises

63

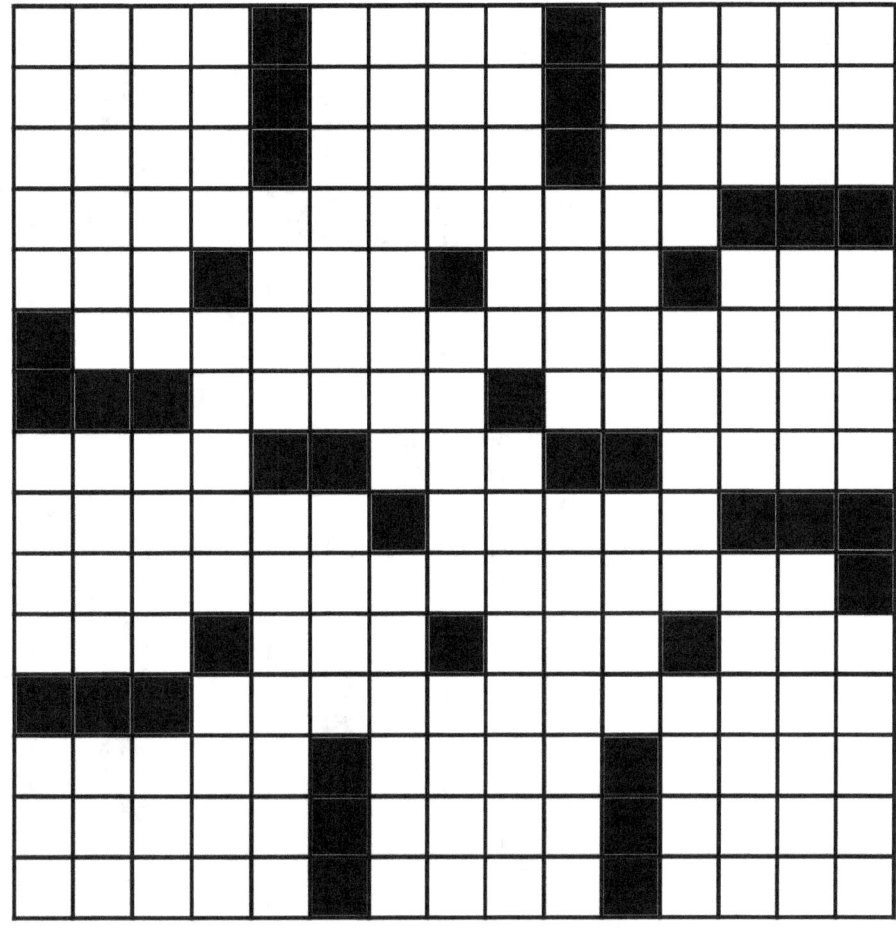

3 Letter
Ape
Ash
Cat
Elf
End
Fro
ILO
LAN
Met
Pen
Rho
Rpm
Sol
Son
USA

4 Letter
Case
Coho
Data
Dons
Eddy
Enol
Fino
Goon
Gory
Herd
Iran
Leek
Lire
Loci
Mesa
Ocas
Olds
Olio
Omen
Only
Opal
Open
Roar
Rocs
Role

Salt
Slam
Slid
Tout
Your

5 Letter
Ashen
Carpi
Copse
Elude
Ensky
Human
Islet
Romps
Roses
Syrup
Thong
Tiger
Wrong

6 Letter
Amends
Casino
Desist
Mailed
Noodle
Operon
Spaded
Trinal

7 Letter
De-icing
Scholar
Slogans
Utensil

8 Letter
Flamenco
Licensee

12 Letter
Octogenarian
Primogenitor

14 Letter
No-win situation
Sergeant at arms

64

3 Letter

Aga
Ate
Bel
Ear
Ens
Hes
Huh
Its
Lac
Lea
Mar
Oca
One
Out
Psi
Pun
Rap
Rio
Sos
Tow

5 Letter

Apace
Conte
Elite
Enemy
Obese
Op art
Peels
Stare
Udder
Usage

6 Letter

Agaric
Asleep
Behest
Cycads
Dynast
Greedy
Instep
Larges
Norman
Pseudo
Redraw
Refill
Rosets
Script
Spirit

Spuing
Stairs
Stones
Tuxedo
Vamped

7 Letter

Aeonian
Anthrax
Banally
Cetacea
Dessert
Ebonies
Entrain
Genoese
Iceboat

Ideated
Imagery
Italian
Nesters
Plashed
Reapers
Related
Seriate
Terence
Tiering
Vanuatu

65

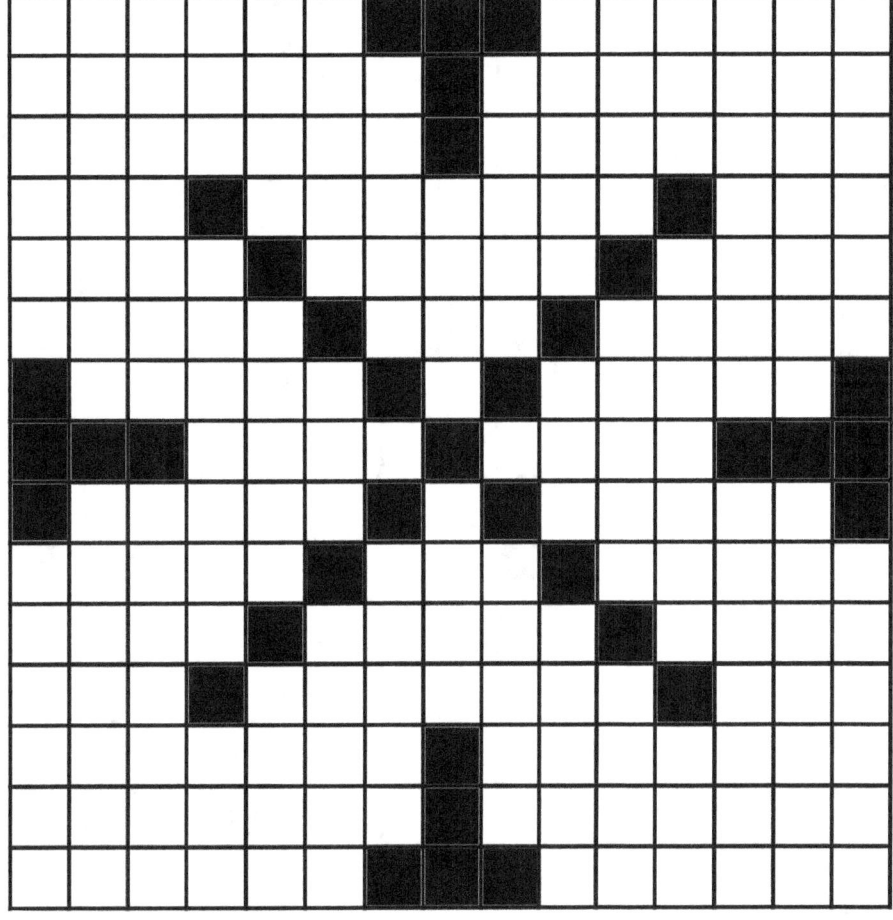

3 Letter
Arm
Art
Ira
Kea
Kin
Nil
Phi
Ray
RNA
Rod
Sol
Sos

4 Letter
Acts
Door
Dorm
Flip
Head
Hole
John
Prim
Tael
Team
Tory
Upon

5 Letter
Chevy
Chino
Cloth
Cooee
Éclat
Ester
Groan
Hooey
Ledge
Opera
Other
Peeve
Relax
Share

Shoot
Slang
Starr
Stern
Strop
Track

6 Letter
Angina
Carats
Cognac
Dynamo
Shasta
Strand
Xmases
Yeasts

7 Letter
Apricot
Aspirin
Choosey
Earnest
Gherkin
Glorias
Graters
Hardpan
Lottery
Nearing
Operate
Pharaoh
Realtor
Release
Roaming
Rookies
Seafood
Skipper

Tinhorn
Upended

66

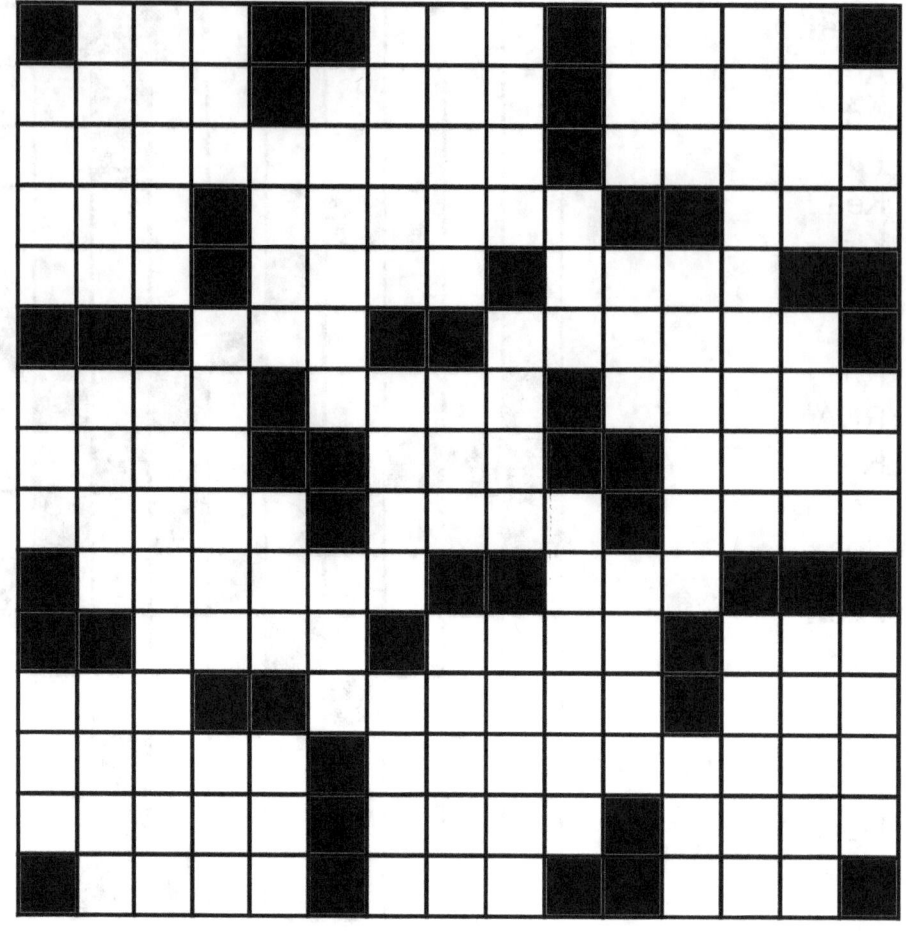

3 Letter
Add
Any
Are
Ate
Cur
Did
Dim
Don
Ebb
Emu
Ill
Imp
Lei
Nay
Ode
Pod
Pun
Roe
Rye
Sac
Sew
Soy
Sty
Tip
War
Web
Wee
You

4 Letter
Acme
Afar
Airy
Alms
Berg
Came
Demo
Digs
Earn
Espy
Ewer
Guru
Hide
Ibis
Into
Iris
Leer
Love
Meet
More
Nova
Oath
Op-ed
Pale
Plus
Scam
Span
Urea

5 Letter
Alibi
Angry
Boots
Bruit
Cubic
Denim
Doyen
Edema
Emcee
Emery
Endow
Paean
Scary
Waver

6 Letter
Caliph
Clergy
In situ
Mutual
Nuance
Oilcan
Sit-ups
Tunnel

9 Letter
Ambiguous
Eyeshadow
Face saver
Regarding

67

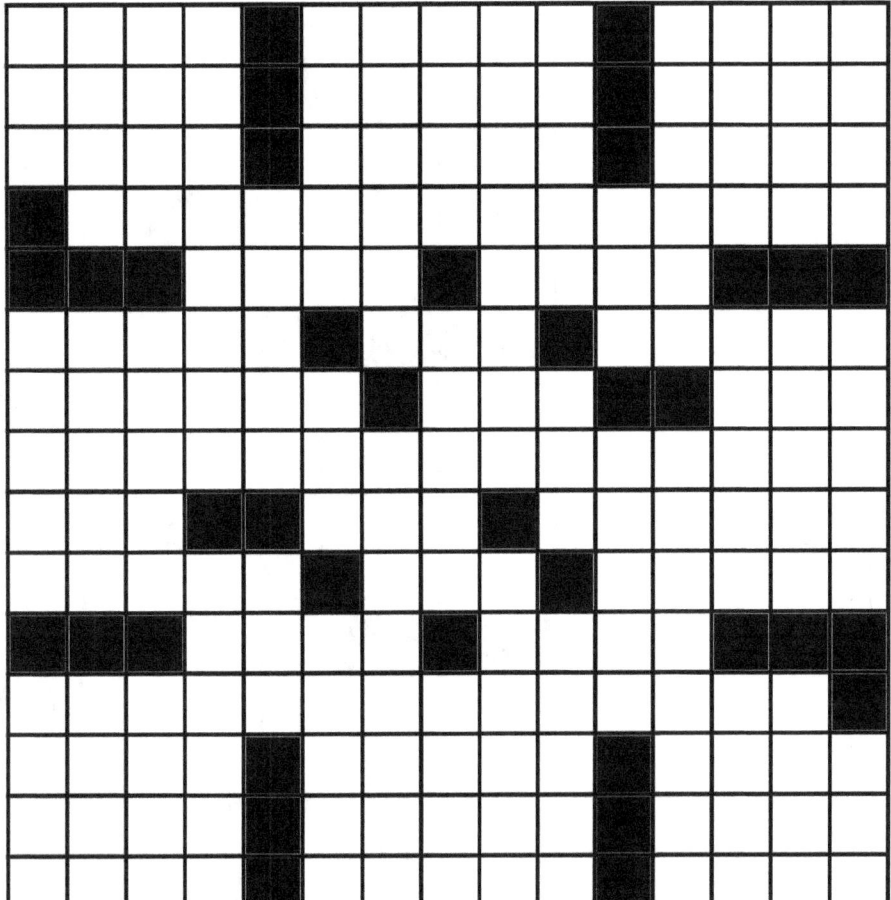

3 Letter
Aye
Ens
Fob
Gov
Imp
Koi
Owe
Pry
Ref
Rib
Ski
Yam

4 Letter
Anna
Arco
Been
Clue
Edam
Eden
Eked
Et al
Flea
Holy
Icky
Idle
Inst
Leis
Mega
Mosh
Ogre
Okay
Oreo
Owed
Raga
Real
Refs
Ruts
Scar
Seer
True
Ugli

5 Letter
Agama
Antic
Becks
Bytes
Cease
Edema
Enact
Enure
Ethic
Event
Ewers
Hindu
Inner
Irate
Least
Nimby
Sotho
Telic

Togas
Trait
Unset
Wotan
Yahoo

6 Letter
Donate
Earner
Eludes
Hokier
Martyr
Yeoman

8 Letter
Goes home
Load line
Machismo
Sentient

14 Letter
Natural history
Rocket launcher

15 Letter
Chattel mortgage

68

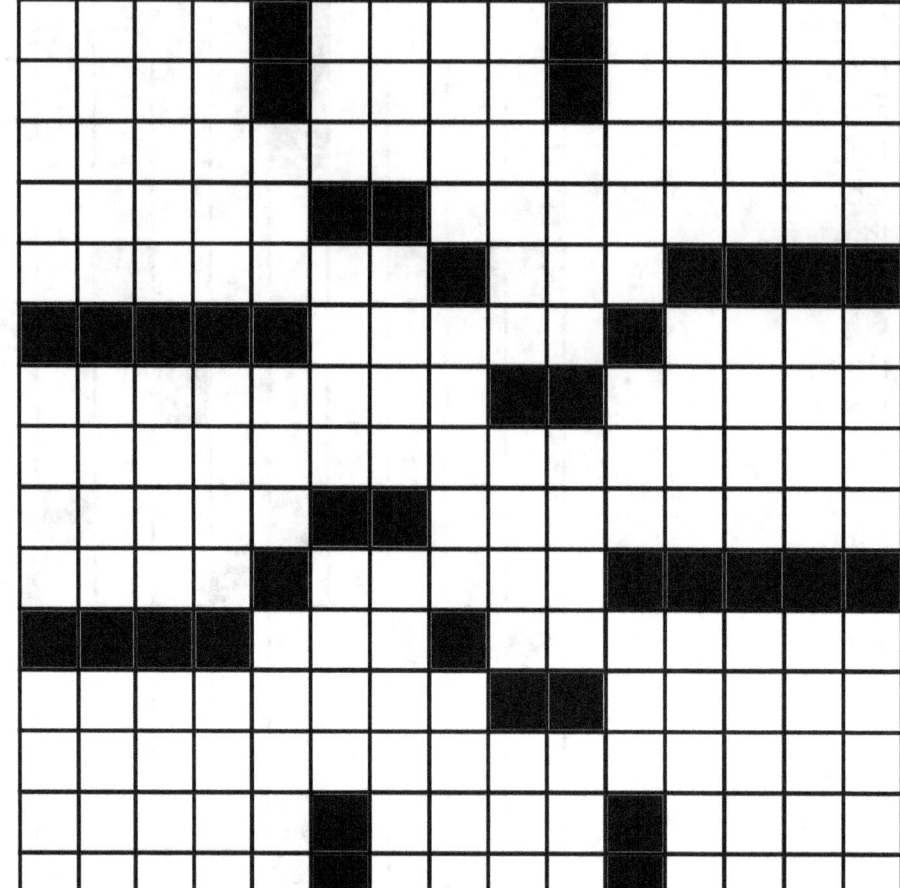

3 Letter
CRT
E'en
Its
Kay
Oho
Pal
Pan
Sow
Tan
Vim

4 Letter
Ache
Ahem
Alms
Ashy
Boot
Data
Dull
Elms
Ergo
Esau
Eyes
Guam
Halo
Hera
Hoer
Idea
Imam
Itch
Lest
Link
Lots
Nipa
Oahu
Oath
Olio
Ones
Retd
Sago
Scam
Seta

Shay
Slit
Spas
Vert

5 Letter
Agist
Alkie
Alone
Antre
Cacao
Cosec
Faith
Kempt
Month
Moots
Mosey
Nests
Oakum
Oldie

Olive
Outgo
Pacts
Pails
Pecan
Poesy
Shaft

6 Letter
Sudoku
Unease

7 Letter
Ottoman
Toehold

8 Letter
Isolated
Moussaka
Noisette
Protrude

15 Letter

Acknowledgement
 In the same
breath
 Male chauvinists

69

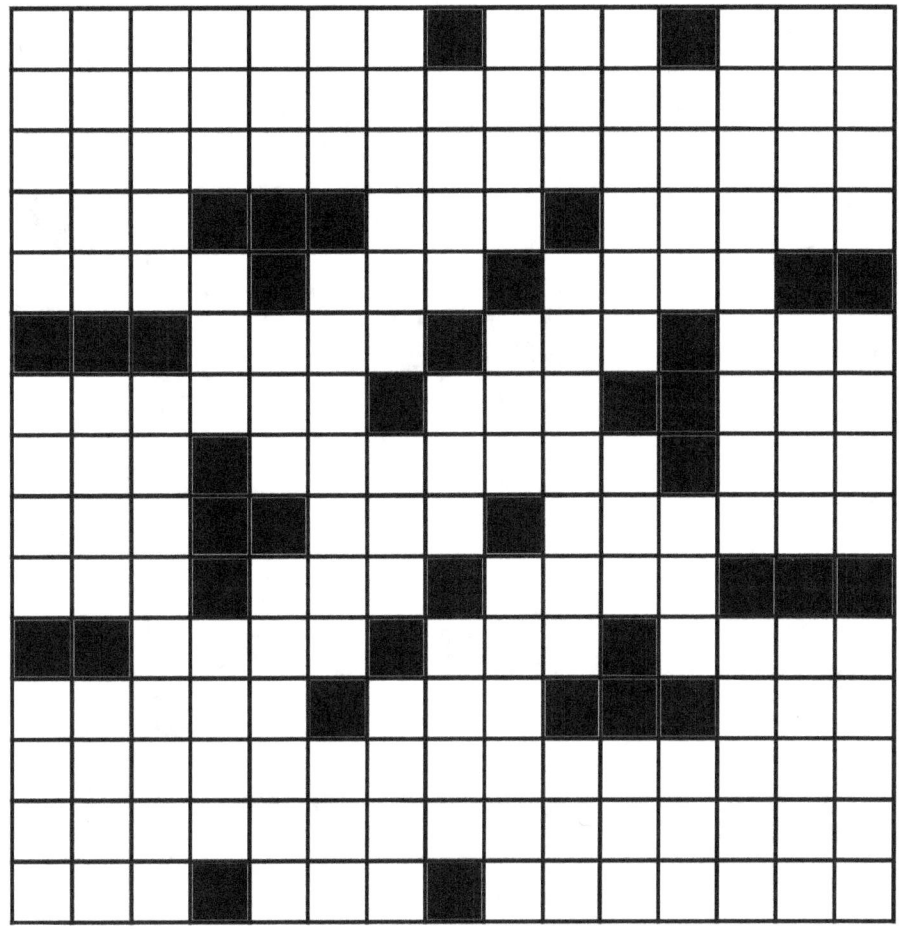

3 Letter
Act
Baa
Boy
Cep
CIA
Cue
Den
Ere
EST
Eta
Fay
Few
Foe
GSA
Hue
Ids
Ill
Ire
Its
Lac
Lei
Lop
Lot
New
Nth
Ono
Pal
Sac
Spa
TNT
Tom
Try
Use
Yes
Yuk

4 Letter
Ales
Also
Aria
Bema
Cere
Deep
Evil
Fern
Iffy
Lute
Naan
Ness
Posy
Shed
Swob
Taco
Tear
Ulna
Year

Yoga

5 Letter
Beths
Elate
Ictus
Ounce
Sails
Tepid
Terse
Wheel

6 Letter
Analog
Congos
Guitar
Inside
Kinsey
Snarfs

7 Letter
Begonia
Freight
Polemic
Staples
Tetanic

9 Letter
Accoutres
Disinfect

15 Letter
Electropositive
Fertile Crescent
Freedom of speech
Parthenogenesis

70

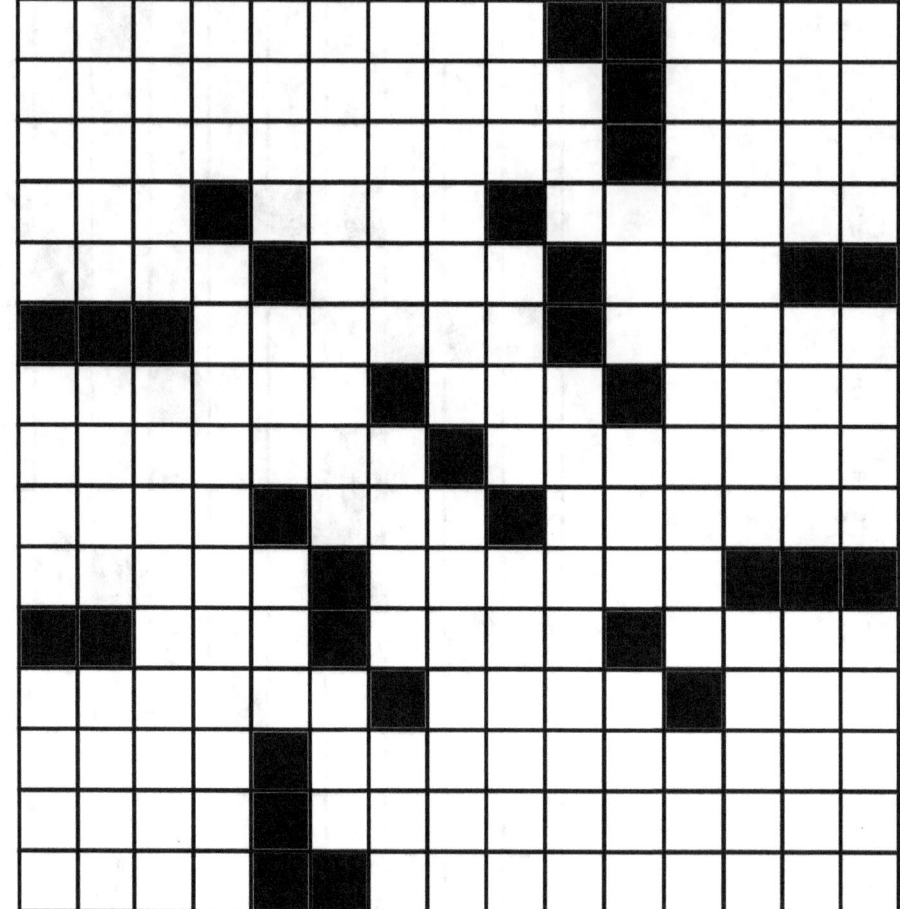

3 Letter
Amp
Ant
Did
Eat
EEC
Err
Eve
Lea
Lei
Leo
Mat
Nil
Old
Pal
Sea
Set

4 Letter
Anoa
Asci
Bawl
Cued
Digs
Dreg
Eddo
Esau
Evil
Gaud
Goal
Lust
Lute
Nisi
Offs
Pang
Rigs
RISC
Roil
RSVP
Sari

Song
Tied
Tsar
User
Wats

5 Letter
Cords
Fence
Flint
Glenn
Obeli
On ice
Sages
Vapor

6 Letter
Alkali
Beetle
Gigolo
Gnosis
Laredo
Lasers
Pedant
Varese

7 Letter
Averted
Diorama
Etagere
Pupated

9 Letter
Cassettes
Deselects
Eulogists
Insatiate
Intrusted
Vocatives

10 Letter
Abominates
Perpetrate
Reassuming
Remittance

11 Letter
Clarinetist
Rat kangaroo

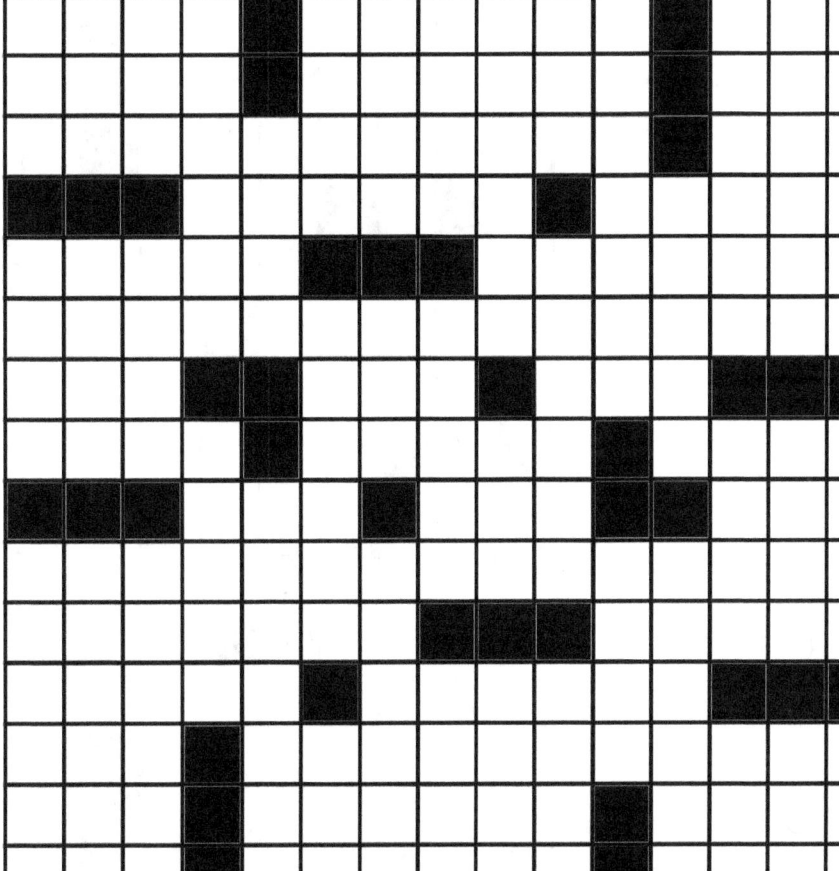

3 Letter
Act
Ana
Ape
Arm
Ave
Can
Etc
Fie
Ire
It'd
Led
Lei
Neo-
Ova
Pit
Pol
She
Ted
Tee
Tsp
Use
Was

4 Letter
Acme
Alas
Asti
Awes
Chid
Duel
Each
Eden
Erst
Into
Lame
Late
Name
Noir
Sass

Secs
Sera
Shia
Spat
Thou

5 Letter
Alias
Apses
CD-ROM
Mails
Racer
Scram
Seine
Uncle

6 Letter
Anemia
Apollo
Clamps
Decors
Earful
Elapse
Emceed
Eterne
Hawaii
Layers
Liaise
Mantic
Nutmeg
Osprey
Panama
Rudest
Selsyn

Wapiti

7 Letter
Aimless
Eternal
Ineptly
Siamese

11 Letter
Impedimenta
Narcoleptic

15 Letter
Electromagnetic
Panel
discussion

72

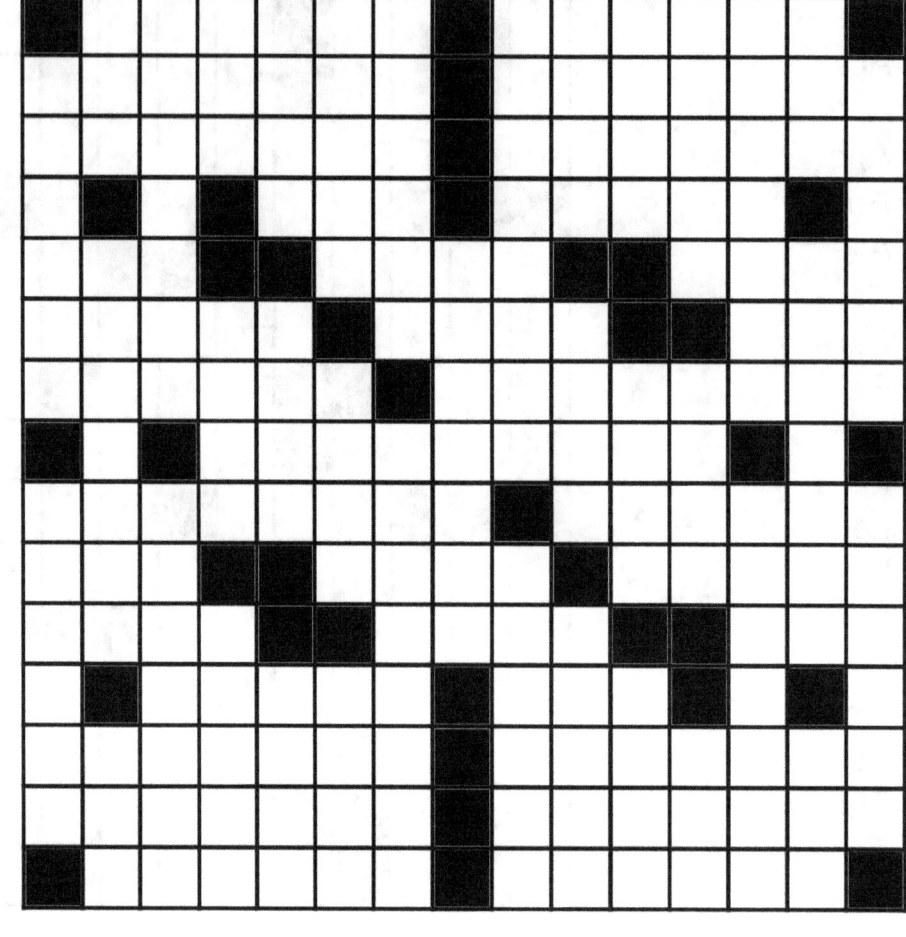

3 Letter
Aba
Bee
Dad
Gas
GMT
GPO
Had
Inn
Lea
Nil
Pug
Rod

4 Letter
Acid
Crop
Cyan
Deer
Dual
Erns
Errs
Idol
Iota
Lark
Nine
Over
Psst
Rape
Shul
Stet
USSR
Vela

5 Letter
Adieu
Asper
House
No-hit
Oaten
Rainy
Tonal
Torsi

6 Letter
Bagdad
Bright
Dalasi
Delete
Deltas
Karsts
Merely
Recoup
Strand
System
Tiptop
Tishri

7 Letter
Arduous
Bermuda
Erratum
In store
Nirvana
Odonata
Parapet
Poisons
Protégé
Redtail
Sheathe
Sorcery
Tie beam
Tighten
Uterine

8 Letter
Emaciate
Recovery
Repartee
Toilsome

9 Letter
Undeceive

73

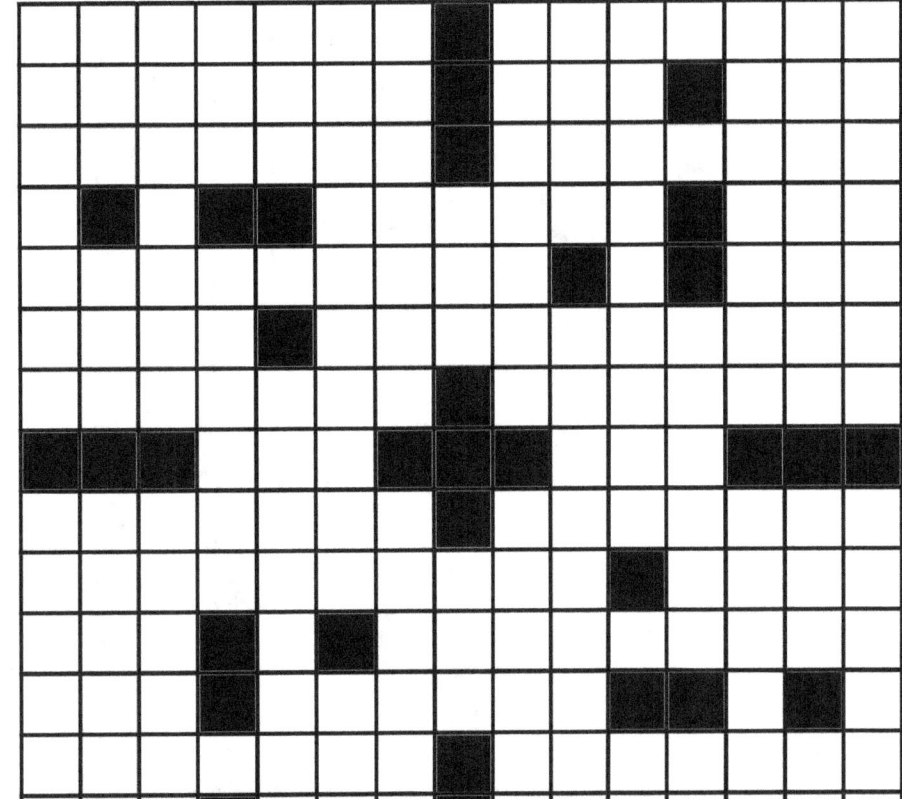

3 Letter
Ace
All
Are
Ear
E'en
Era
Her
I've
Leo
Min
Ode
Ort
Pen
Pip
Roe
Rug
Tea
Ten
Tor
USA

4 Letter
Apex
Asea
Gaud
Hath

6 Letter
Iguana
Isobar
Shares
Stream

7 Letter
Bahamas
Bernini
Borscht
Creeper
Epigeal
Epitome
E-tailer
Externs
Fitness
Foresee
Hastate
Heroine
Indulge
Lawless
Lubbers
Ocarina
Precede
Resents
Sassier
Scherzi
Schlepp
Scleras
Silvern
Sine die
Speller
Spinets
Suttees
Treater

9 Letter
Cease-fire
Detriment
Torchiere
Warrantor

10 Letter
Antifreeze
Autocratic
Crescentic
Retransmit

74

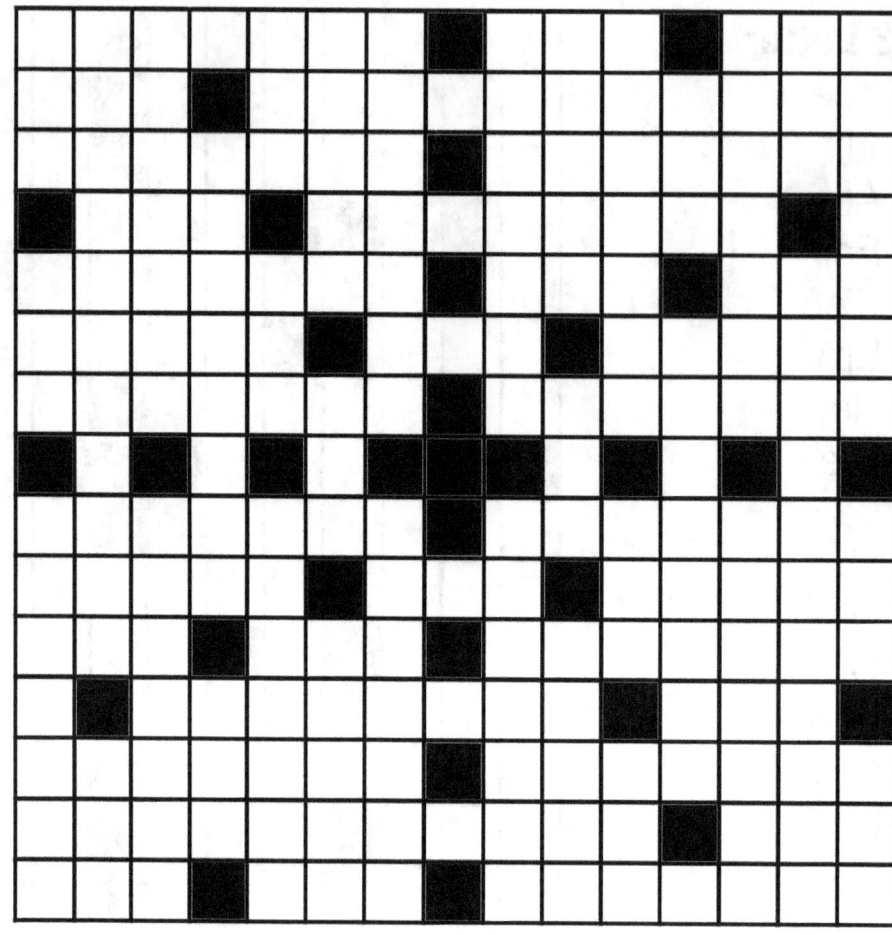

3 Letter
Aha
Ani
Ate
Bed
Car
DNA
Edo
Eel
Eon
Gag
Hit
Hod
Hue
Ira
Lam
Mad
Mas
Neo-
Rat
Set
Sew
She
Son
Sty
Tar
Too
Tsp
USA

5 Letter
Adore
Aruba
Chyme
Nukes
Offer
Opted
Orion
Scape

7 Letter
Aground
At stake
Despond
Dressed
Echelon
Eclairs
Elaters
Enabler
Encores
Enforce
Esteems
Foresaw
Harness
Hymnody
Iron out
Legroom
Maranta

Negated
Peridot
Resorts
Ride out
Rose oil
Santa Fe
Tamable

8 Letter
Escapist
Felo-de-se
Narrator
Tone poem

11 Letter
Gutta-percha
Radio beacon
Surface mail
Temperature

75

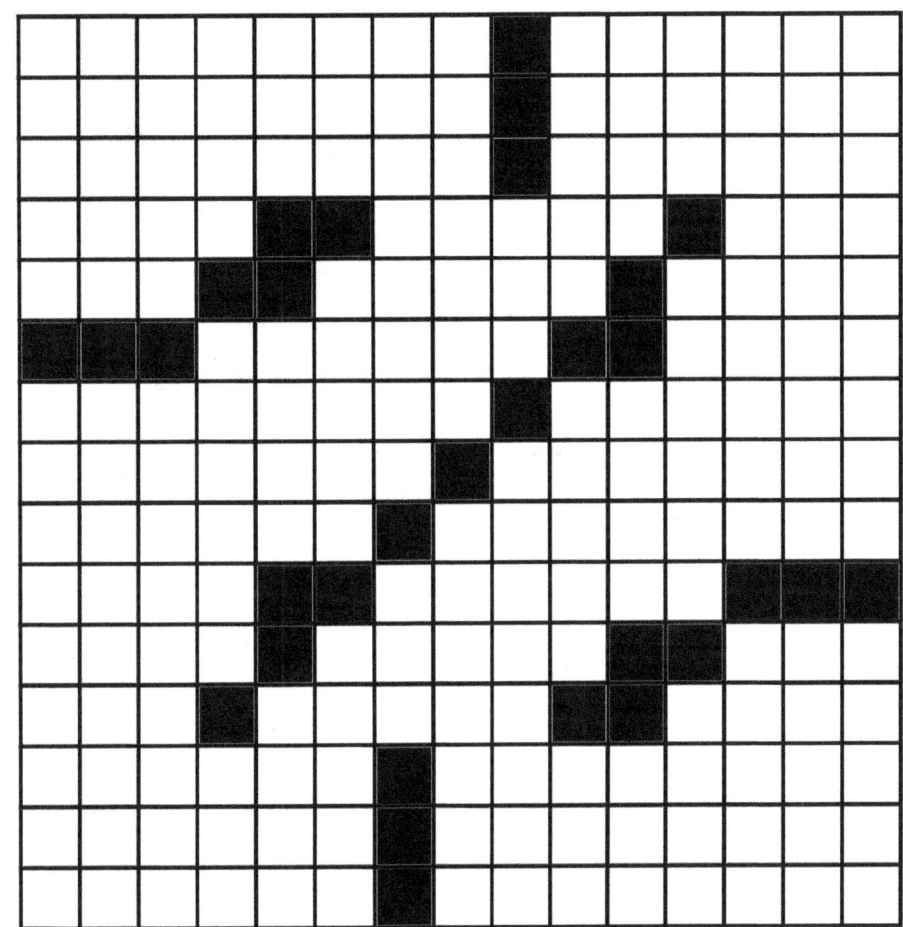

3 Letter
Bra
Bur
Den
Gyp
Her
Ins
Lop
Pen
PhD
Sax
Tsp
Vee

4 Letter
Agra
Arch
Coat
Dude
Eggs
Etch
Levo-
Moil
Near
Tear
Vela
Vice

5 Letter
Adieu
Coney
Decoy
Elude
Fichu
Flees
Lurid
Named
Pupil
Purer
Renal
Rupee
Slung
Uncap

6 Letter
Adverb
Bypass
Calais
Dueler
Earths
Either
Felted
Fontal
Ideate
Relate
Steeve
Terror

7 Letter
Legator
Seducer
Trances
Typical

8 Letter
Area code
Capsicum
Emeritus
Lapidary
Lonesome
Lynx-eyed
Saboteur
Scuttles
Tangiers
Uncapped

9 Letter
Aragonite
Barrister
Breathers
Elaborate
Retractor
Steamiest

76

3 Letter
Ado
Ape
Cup
Dab
Dug
Gem
Hem
Lee
Neo-
Oak
Ode
One
Ore
Pan
Phi
Psi
Rah
Rev
Var
Yak

4 Letter
Aver
Bast
East
Eden
Esau
Grip
Lego
Nags
Onto
Pleb
Sacs
Siam
Sigh
Snob
Stye
Yelp

5 Letter
Burka
Cheat
Ideal
Lumps
Radio
Rices
Sopor
Tonic

6 Letter
Bedamn
Donkey
Edgers
Modest
Scoots
Statal

7 Letter
Adaptor
At least
Biodata
Bipolar
Delouse
El Greco
Erratic
Ignobly
Kaisers
Layette
Lighten
Missile
Name tag
Noticed
Orlando
Sea dogs
Ski pole

Solvers
Steroid
Tableau
Tapered
Triadic
Up to par
Usurped

8 Letter
Dunce cap
Malamute

77

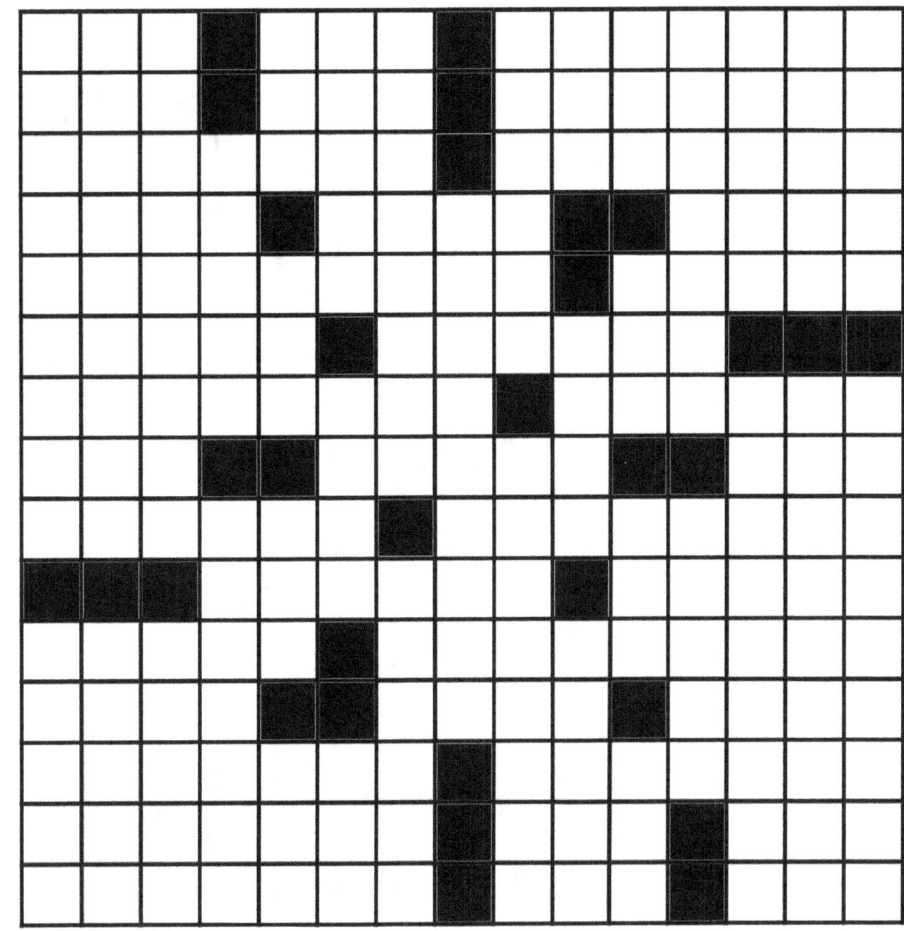

3 Letter
Ark
Bap
BIH
Deo
DSA
Dyn
Ecu
E'er
Ess
Fun
Gnu
IAS
Ili-
ITU
NFT
NTA
Ora
Ovi-
Red
SOR

4 Letter
Anat
FT-SE
Holi
INLA
IPad
Lift
Nerk
Oner

5 Letter
Aleft
Ethyl
Flics
Grise
Kilps
Kombu
Maror
Nguni
Nifty
Ollas
Op art
Or ere
Sitar
Strag
Teles

6 Letter
Ephebe
Eraser
Lasing
Nudism
Uckers
Waveys

7 Letter
Avenger
Laridae
Offside
Proverb
Snashes
Strooke
Sub divo
Ungorg'd
Virgule

Woe unto

8 Letter
Epanodos
Pistolet
Tziganes
Ypsiloid

9 Letter
Asafetida
Dislustre
Indianise
Masseters
Point-lace
Sanitizer
Smasheroo
Stoccados
Uterotomy

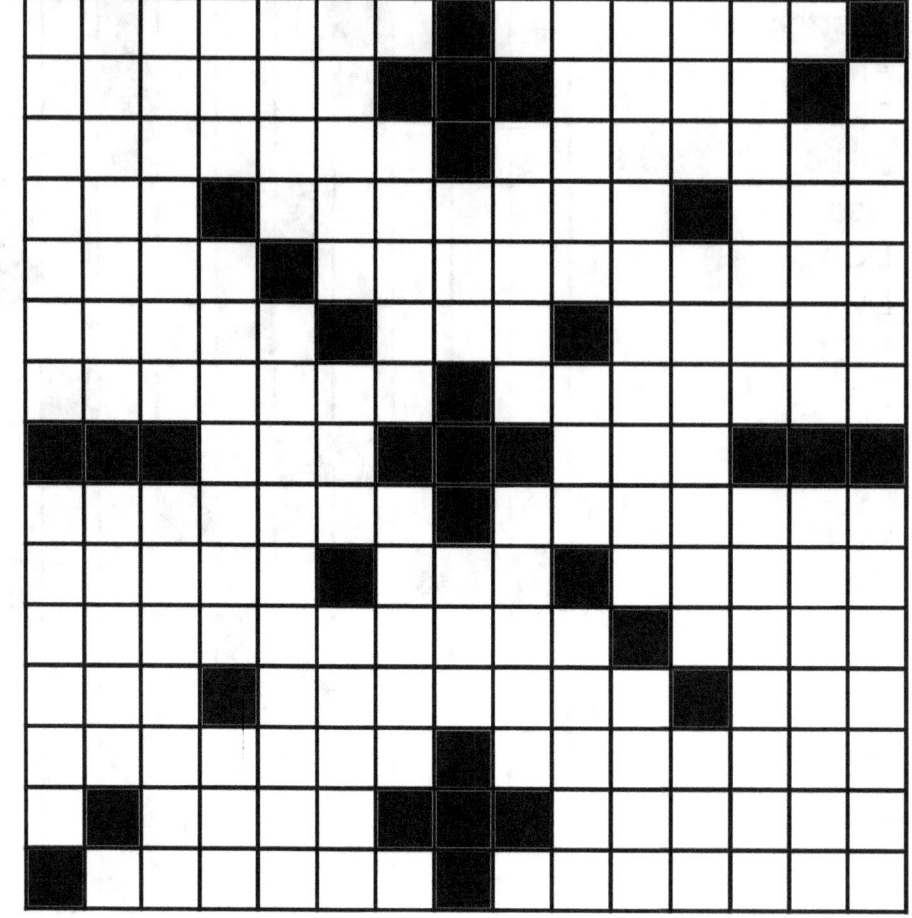

3 Letter
Ate
Cue
Dim
Ego
Ems
EST
Fop
Gin
Hem
Ire
Lit
Orr
Psi
Tat
Ten
Wee

4 Letter
Dams
Drop
Laic
Suer
Tear
Tref

5 Letter
Apter
Arête
Coach
Cream
Drawl
Erect
Estop
Extra
Fetes
Murre
Niche

Samba
Tromp
Udder

6 Letter
Access
Berths
Cupful
Reseat
Stereo
Uprear

7 Letter
Adoptee
Appease
Attests
Baghdad
Bustles
Caftans
Cowpeas
Foolish
Granita
Hermits
Iced tea
Moonlit
Retorts
Seawall
Shaitan

Spammed
Spectra
Stretti
Striped
Subtext
Tensest
Up to par

10 Letter
Consummate
Ear trumpet
Pass muster
Production

79

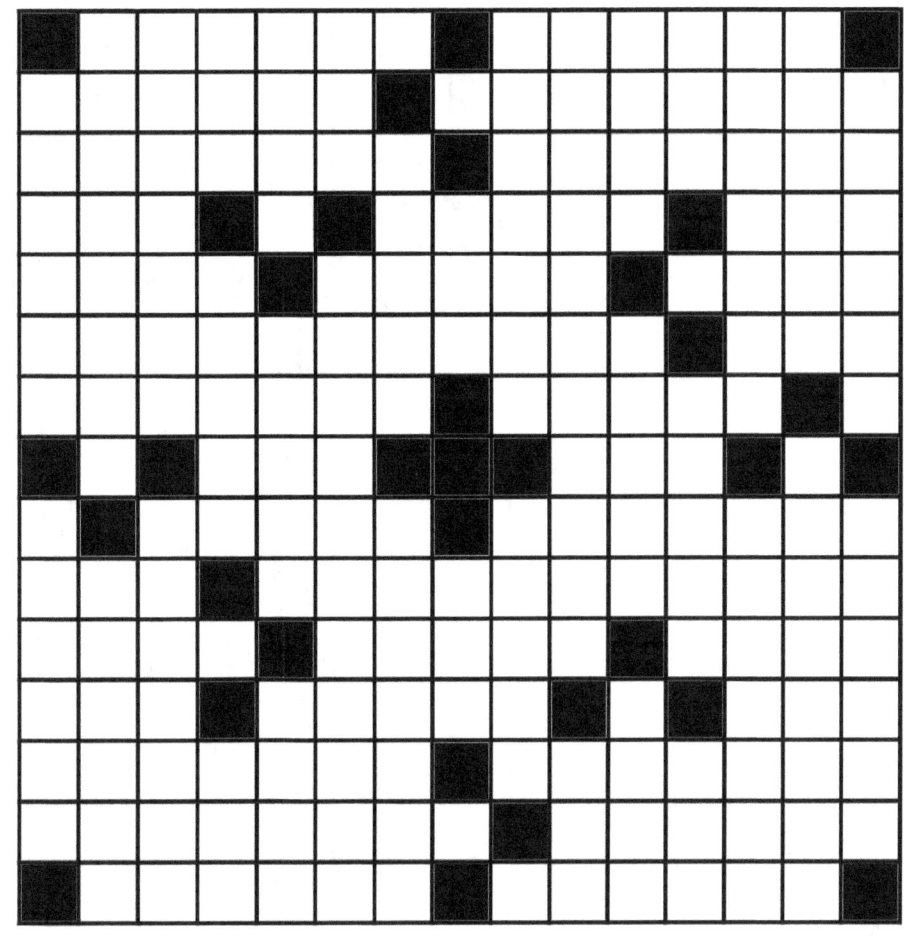

3 Letter
Ace
Act
DNA
Dup
Eel
EST
Goa
Ice
Irk
Its
Nan
Oar
Ohm
Ted
Ten
Yak

4 Letter
Anti
Asci
Exit
Iron
Omen
Rube
Scud
Side

5 Letter
Aahed
Arced
Beast
Easts
Ewers
Nylon
Peats
Recur
Scuds
Shoal
Untie

Wylie

6 Letter
Caress
Conoid
Edison
Except
Reeded
Scions
Sedate
Senile
Snatch
Steads
Typify
Zenana

7 Letter
Chelsea
Consume
Dankest
Dead set
Ebbtide
Erectly
Sardine
Sea star
Shinned
Sutlers
Tuition
Unitary

8 Letter
Enormous
Gardenia
Sprucely
Thrushes

11 Letter
Arbitrageur
Barrier reef
Nosy-parkers
Sericulture

80

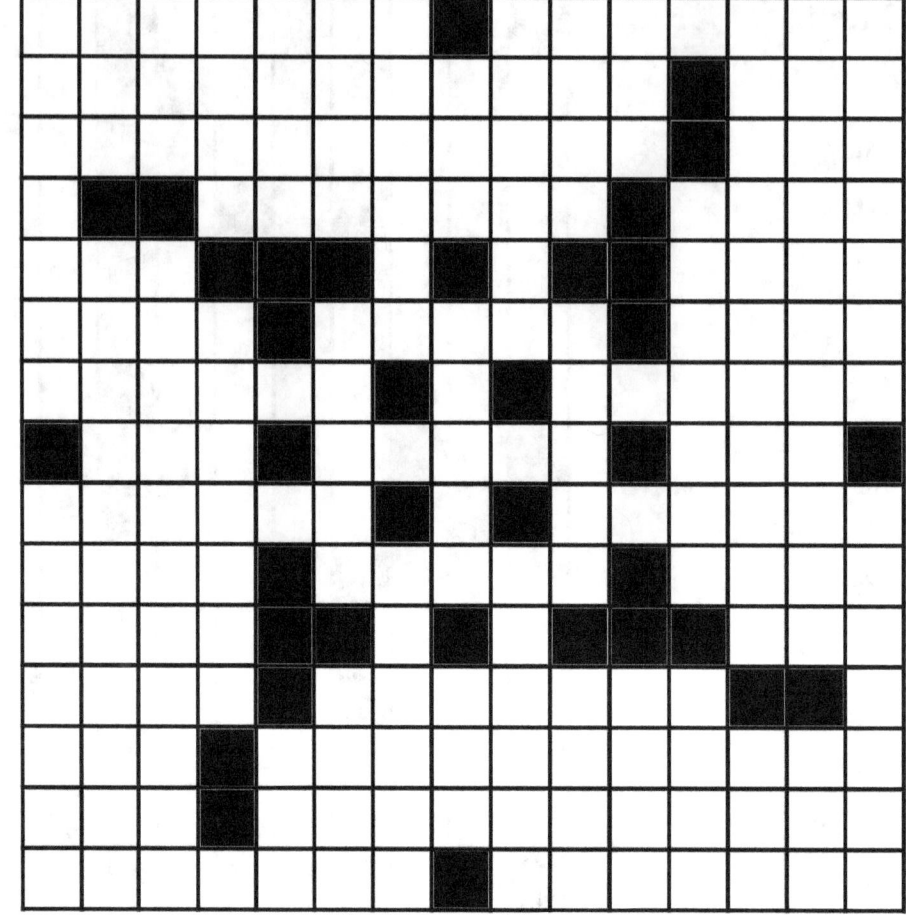

3 Letter
Arp
Ash
Asp
Bin
Dud
ENE
Get
GNP
Led
Min
Nun
Ova
Pry
Rad
Tad
Tot

4 Letter
Aden
Aril
Bema
Date
Et al
Gene
Here
Isis
Limo
Loom
Node
Pact
Peen
Scad
Tsar
Ulna

5 Letter
Basra
Crimp
NAACP
Nisei
Xebec
Xenon

6 Letter
Atonal
Chemic
Enlace
Merino
Monied
Pledge
Rancor
Unsafe

7 Letter
Calends
Deadpan
Dryness
Gone bad
Madison
Milages
Pennant
Rattler
Smash-up
Smuggle
Strudel
Up to par

11 Letter
Avocado pear
Denumerable
Miscellanea
Nonresident
Polarimeter
Potato crisp
Unanimities
Unharnessed

81

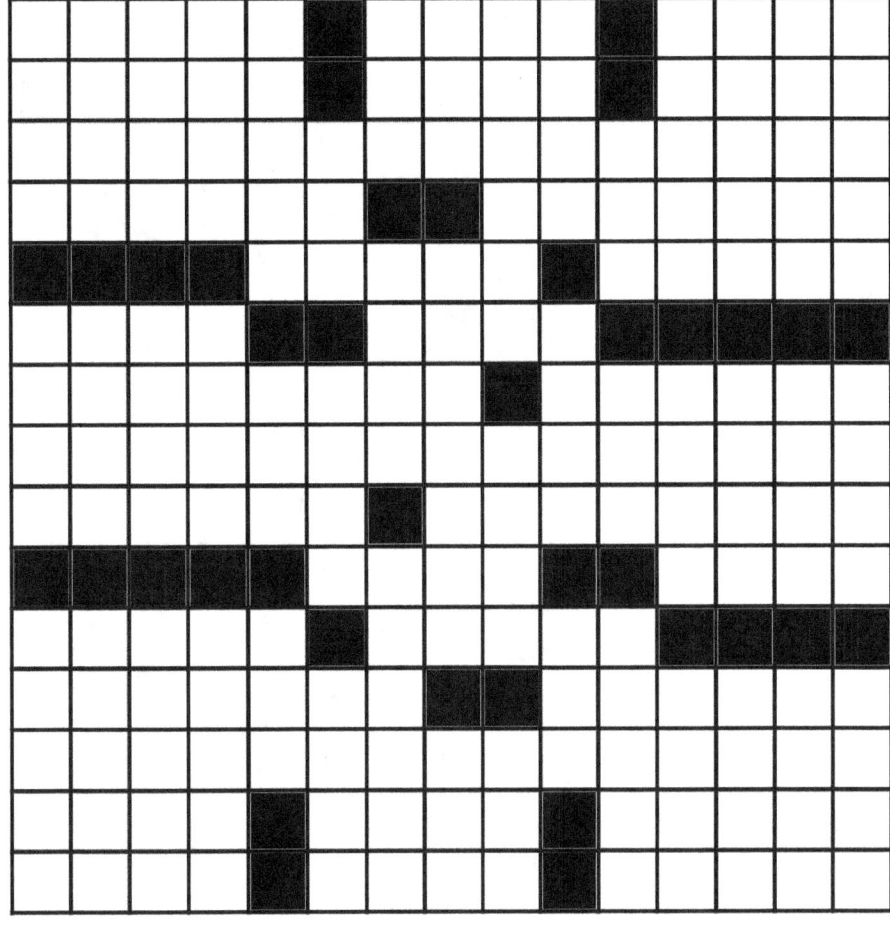

3 Letter
Air
CBS
Dah
Ens
Lea
LSD
Ode
Ply
Tag
Ton

4 Letter
Afro
Alto
Asea
Asps
Cedi
Ceil
Crag
Deco
Edda
Eden
Ends
Épée
Gnat
Guns
Herd
Idle
Inca
It'll
Naif
Ness
Ohms
Once
OPEC
Otic
Psst
Sere
Slat
So-so
Stab
Stem
This
Tolu
Toon
With

5 Letter
Abbés
Adapt
Aegis
Alert
Alter
Bursa
Diode
Egest
Erase
Paste
Plane
Salsa
Skimp
Smote
Spunk
Stela
Tonal
Yalta

6 Letter
Arcing
Diadem
Enlist
Psyche
Sesame
Toecap

7 Letter
Billowy
Dollars
Theorem

8 Letter
Notecase
Remedies

15 Letter
Botanical garden
Cold-bloodedness
Pencil sharpener

82

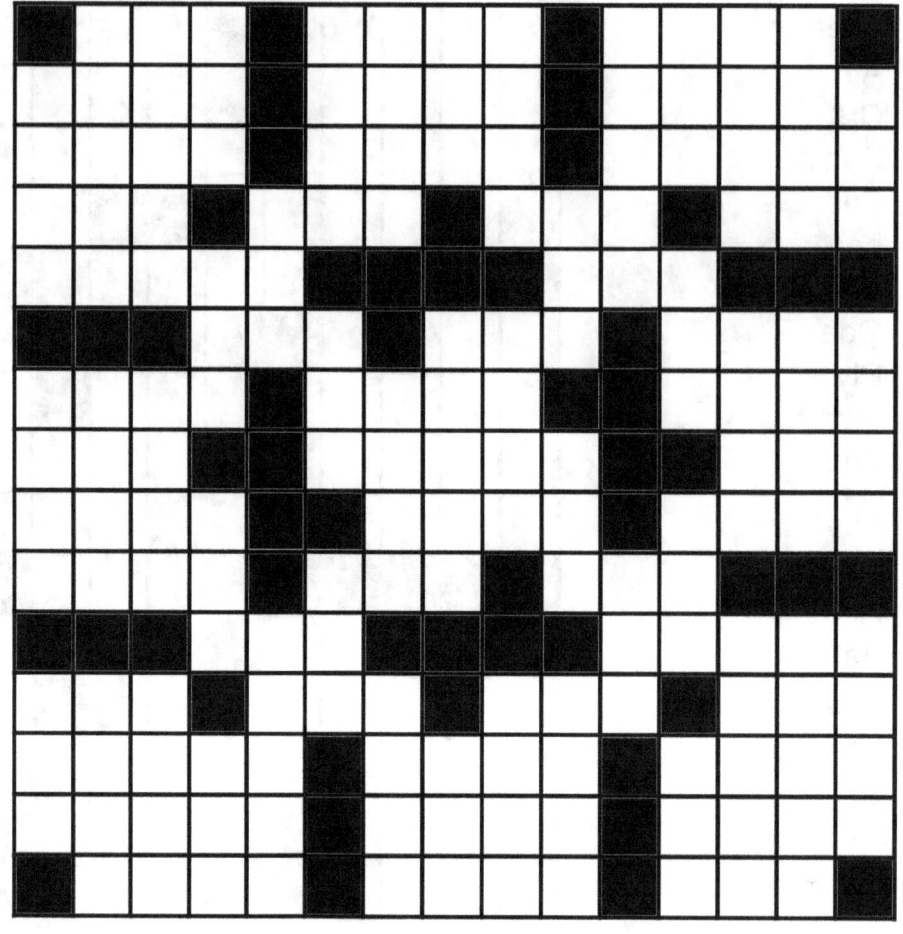

3 Letter
Ace
Ago
Ale
All
Ant
Any
Are
Ash
Aye
Bro
Day
Ebb
Elk
Emu
End
Fog
Gag
Gas
GMT
Her
Him
Hut
Ion
Ken
Kin
Lao
Lei
Nan
Nun
Oca
Ode
Orb
Rho
Sae
Tat
Too

4 Letter
Aden
Asci
Bran
Brio
Coil
Drab
Drum
Emus
Ends
Even
Flea
Fret
Goad
ICAO
Ikon
Kayo
Lava
Levi
Line

Lobe
Loge
Menu
Nail
No-go
Nook
PAYE
Rend
Rest
Retd
Ring
Roll
Slav
Soon
Talc
Test
Tile
Ugli
USPS
Writ

Yawn

5 Letter
Alibi
Balsa
Corer
Ducat
Eerie
Elate
Error
Freya
Neigh
Otter
Ousel
Recce
Tared
Yenta

83

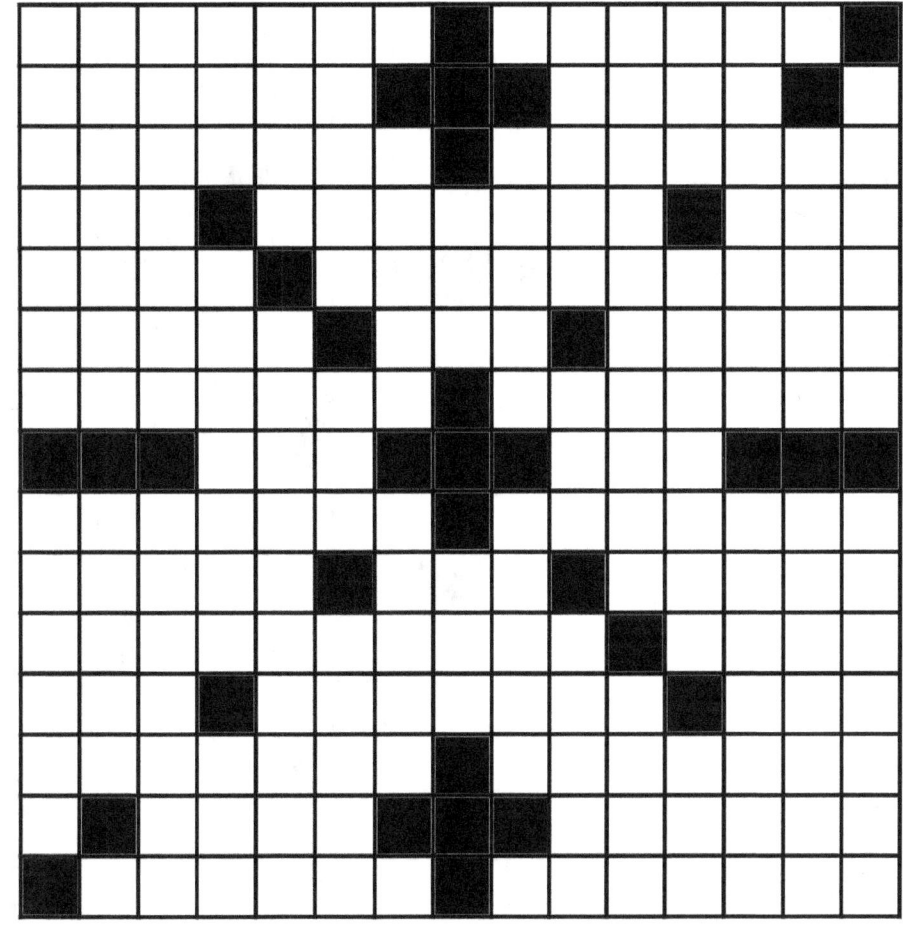

3 Letter
Apr
Arc
Ate
Bum
Ear
E'en
Ice
Lat
Neo-
Net
Ore
Pry
PTA
Ran
Res
Tic

4 Letter
Alar
Edam
Ewer
Meet
Whet
Yale

5 Letter
Avian
DPhil
Drink
Duces
Erose
Error
Event
Lilac
Pulse
Saint
Scuta

Sinai
Twerk
Vista

6 Letter
Attest
Deodar
Oryxes
Regrow
Somali
Tercet

7 Letter
Arabica
Carcase
Decease
Dernier
Emerald
Eremite
Finance
Kuwaiti
Manning
Nomadic
Nursery
Onanist
Pen name
Rapines
Rapture

Scandal
Smetana
Soirées
Solutes
Stipple
Unseals
Useless

10 Letter
Chickenpox
Gingivitis
Identified
Three-piece

84

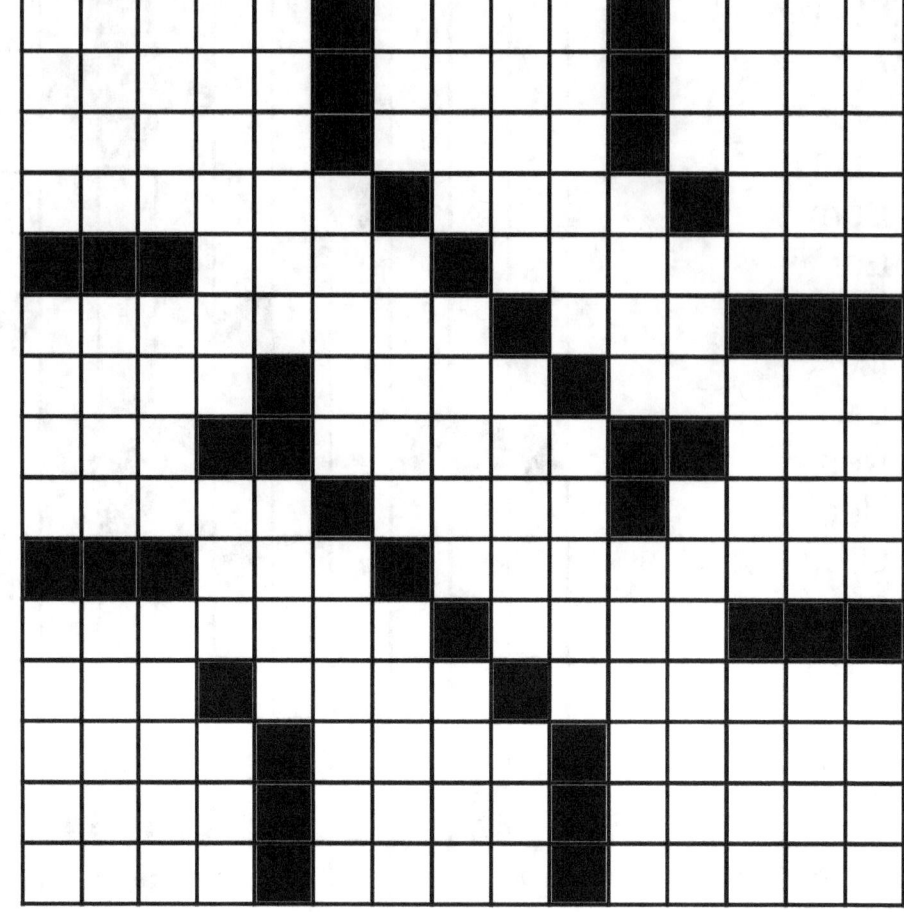

3 Letter
Bid
CGI
Ear
Ego
Eon
Ire
Mrs
Nay
Net
RAF
Rye
Use

4 Letter
Ague
Area
Asti
Boat
Boss
Dual
Duet
Each
Edgy
Erse
Evil
Goof
Hers
Hurl
Ibis
Idol
Inca
Lego
Loan
Loom
Lurk
Mice
Mote
Noir
Onus
Rest
Seal
Sees
Slob
Snip

Sorb
T-bar
Thai
Ursa
Yens
Yuan

5 Letter
Allow
Asian
Bragg
Enure
Erase
Erica
Eyrie
Fagot
Galah
Gigue
Hoo-ha
Keyed
Nauru

Probe
Reeks
Revel
Roble
Saiga
Scalp
Shoal
Soled
Terms

6 Letter
Absorb
Annals
Faulty
Nearer
Ranger
Saloon

7 Letter
Alcohol
Asinine
Kneecap
Poor law

8 Letter
Doorstep
Menorahs

85

3 Letter
Adz
Boa
Con
Cut
Ego
Era
Err
Hay
Hen
Her
Irk
Its
Jar
Lab
Lav
Nan
Nil
Oaf
Old
Ply

4 Letter
Aloe
Amok
Axes
Dana
East
Eked
Elan
Emir
Geld
Gene
Glee
Gyms
Hams
Harm
Kept
Lyon
Olla
Oman
Orcs
Oslo
Pish
Raja

Rest
Rhea
Salk
Slab
Sofa
Taro
Tipi
Toll
Tori
Tree

5 Letter
Befog
Blear
Bliss
Breed
Idyll
Incur
Lathe
Mitts
Roger
Sawer
Smock
Socle
Tiers

6 Letter
Angler
Helios
Inlaid
Invoke
Isobar
Platte

7 Letter
Brittle
Grottos
Midweek

10 Letter
Exhibiting
Gorgonzola
Mercantile
Needlessly
Piano stool
Tonic solfa

86

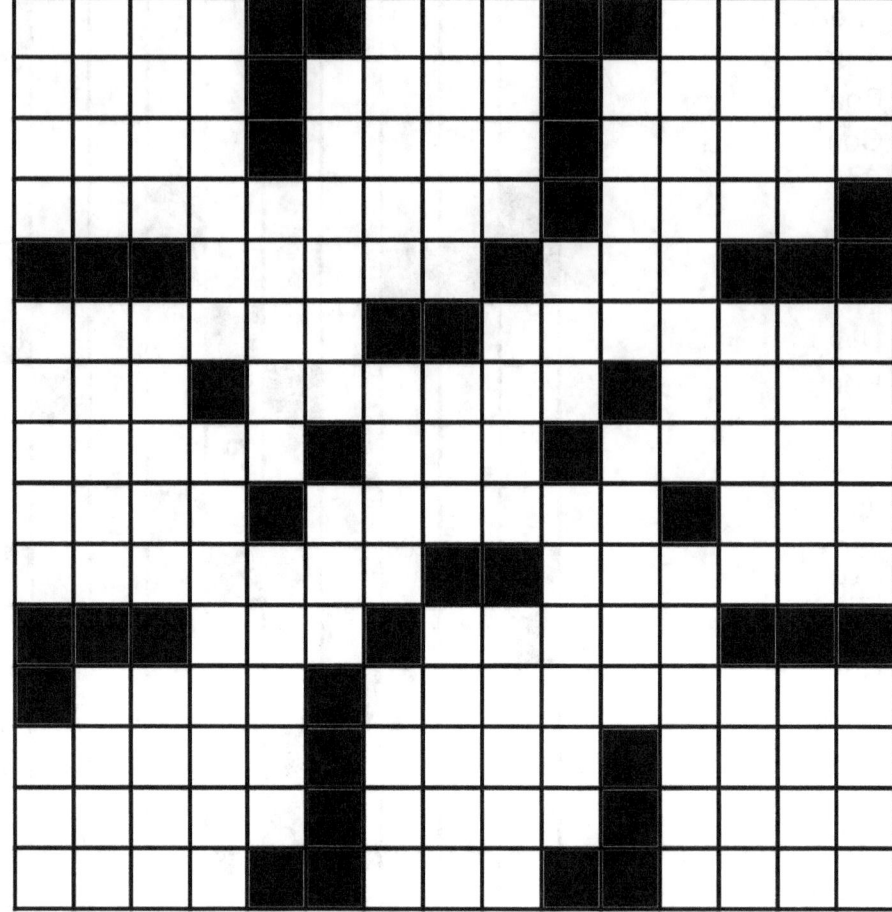

3 Letter
Cog
Eke
FDA
GMT
Lei
Men
O'er
Spa
Tan
Wee
Win
Wry

4 Letter
Adar
Arch
Auto
Axle
Bola
Burl
Chic
Date
Dowd
Dual
Ells
Else
Idol
Ilex
Isis
Lilt
Malt
Mann
Moos
Near
Ocas
Oreo
Pods
Prim
RISC
Roil
Ruse
Sent

Tort
Urea

5 Letter
Acrid
Among
Celeb
Dweeb
Eosin
Forte
Items
Lunge
Macho
Medic
Mouse
Orbit
Owner
Paged
Percy
Ramie

Rodeo
Slued
Sorts
Stack
Unrip
Waddy

6 Letter
Editor
Employ
Ibidem
Obsess
Oodles
Scared
Shrewd
Smudge

7 Letter
Kopecks
Trellis

8 Letter
Ice water
Roman law

9 Letter
Nosepiece
Pool table

87

3 Letter
Ago
Alp
Ani
Apr
Bio
EEC
Ere
Eta
Fee
Lea
Leo
Lie
Mad
New
Nip
NYC
One
Poi
Sir
Ult

4 Letter
Ache
Ambo
Ants
Diet
Eggy
Eire
Elms
Épée
Geez
Lade
Made
Neat
Odor
Pens
Plat
Thud
Tutu
Urea
Wage
Wait

5 Letter
Abets
Adyta
Curia
Étude
Leper
Linum
Ostia
Pitta
Smart
Steer
Tulle
Unite

6 Letter
Adhere
Eluate
Emerge
Encamp
Esteem
Ingots
Lace up
Ottawa
Platte
Pomade
Recipe
Salaam
Shaman
Target
Teemer
Turbit

7 Letter
Poulenc

8 Letter
Crane fly
Ensconce

10 Letter
Postal code
Unfaithful

11 Letter
Temperature
Thunderclap

13 Letter
Zero tolerance

88

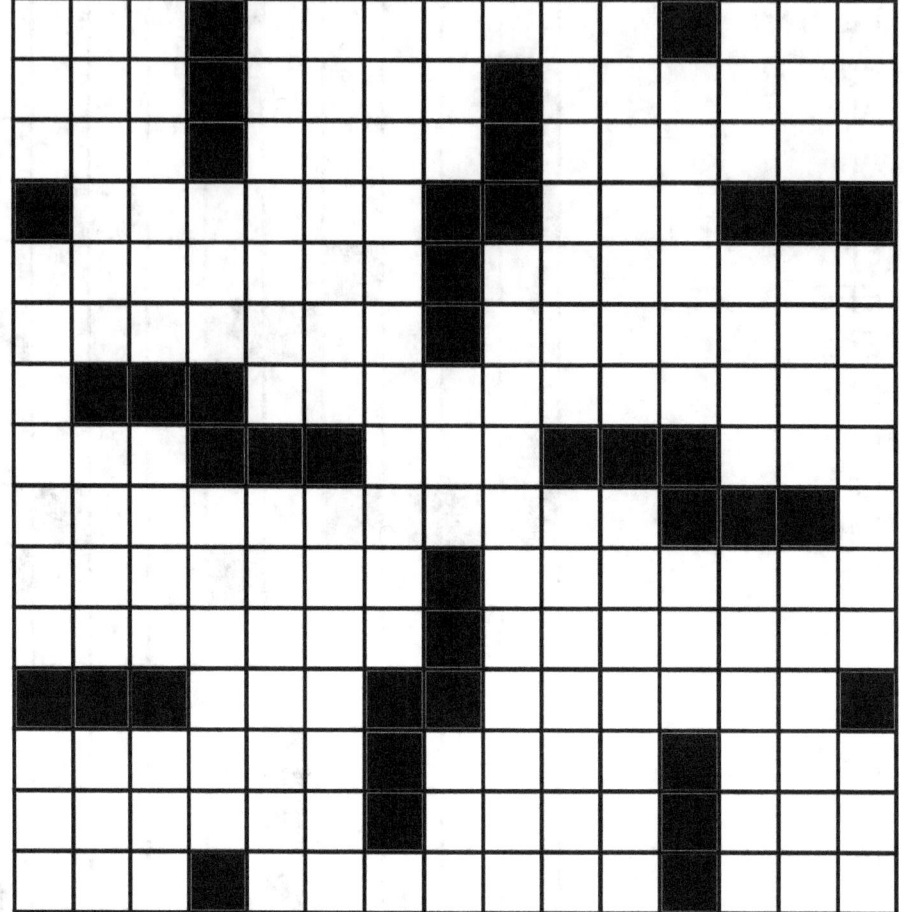

3 Letter
Bus
Dan
Duo
Ego
Ems
ENE
ESP
Ewe
Ira
Its
Nag
Odd
Ode
OTT
Ova
Owe
Pet
Rue
Sin
Tai
Tan
Tea
Ten
Tip
Was
Yaw

4 Letter
Acme
Ahem
Anne
Bade
Cops
Uses
Viol
Writ

6 Letter
Aerate
Dopant
Dustup
Kidder
Laredo
Ortega
Redeye
Renter
Slogan
Tailor
Theist
Tuareg

7 Letter
Abrader
Choosey
Crewels
Dehisce
Dessert
Eats out
Engaged
Everest
Lucerne
Nominee
Obverse
Postwar
Regales
Saclike
Screwed
Sledged
Suborns
Sunrise
Teenage
Uptakes

11 Letter
Eye-watering
Plagioclase
Represented
Rickettsiae

89

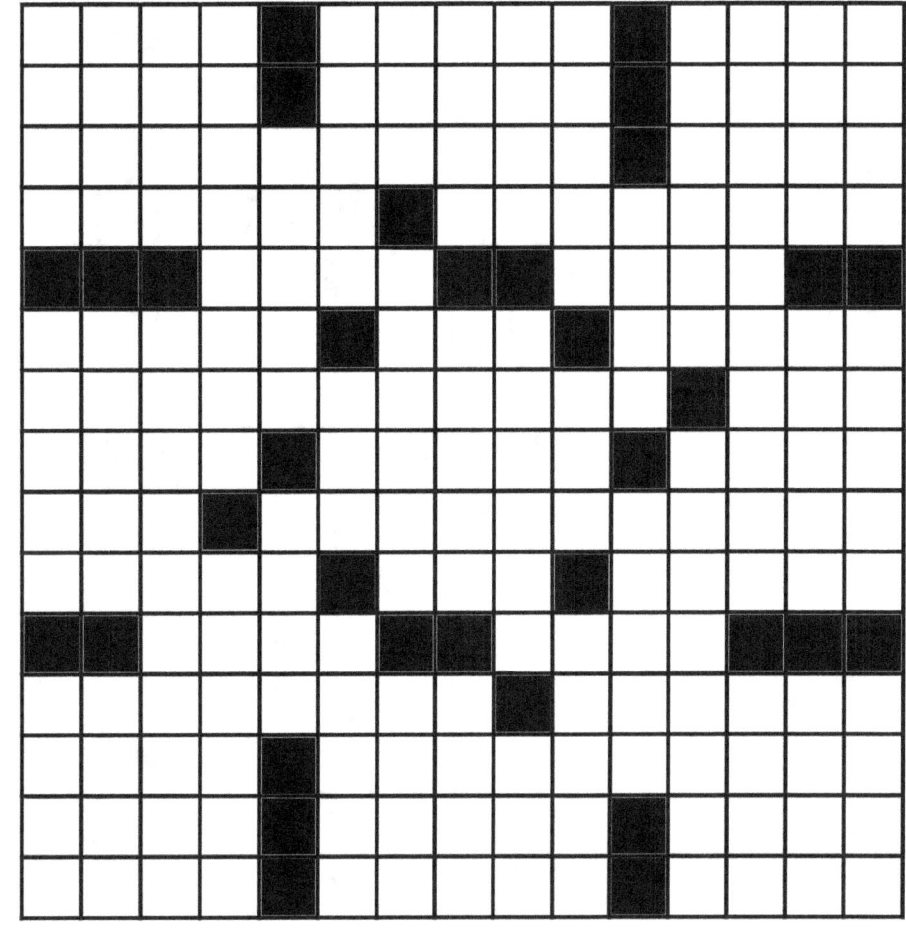

3 Letter
Cap
Gel
Hie
Ido
Lee
Nod
See
Tai

4 Letter
Abel
Apes
Auld
Data
Dose
Drag
East
Ebon
Else
Erin
Gaul
Gees
Horn
Ilia
Ills
Mart
Norm
Robe
Rosa
Roué
Skua
Smug
Snag
Solo
Stay
Stem
Tens
Time
USSR

View
Wadi
Webs

5 Letter
As yet
At sea
Avert
Belie
Deuce
Eerie
Ester
Genoa
Guano
Gutta
Nauru
Obeys
Ogive

On air
Ovule
Rains
Sedum
Spasm
Spoor
Uniat

6 Letter
Ahimsa
Anneal
Decked
Embeds
Sleepy
Versus

8 Letter
Driblets
Internee
Spearmen
Swimming

10 Letter
Admissible
Best seller
Nethermost
Politicked

11 Letter
Goalkeepers
Underinvest

3 Letter
Ace
Dot
Ego
End
Ens
Eon
Err
Lac
Odd
Psi
Reb
Run
Sae
Tar
Tee
Tsp

4 Letter
Acid
Alum
Aria
Mats
Nina
Scum
Tout
Zinc

5 Letter
Aging
Dyers
Elect
EPROM
Irons
Linen
Malay
Onset
Rices
Sense
Snafu

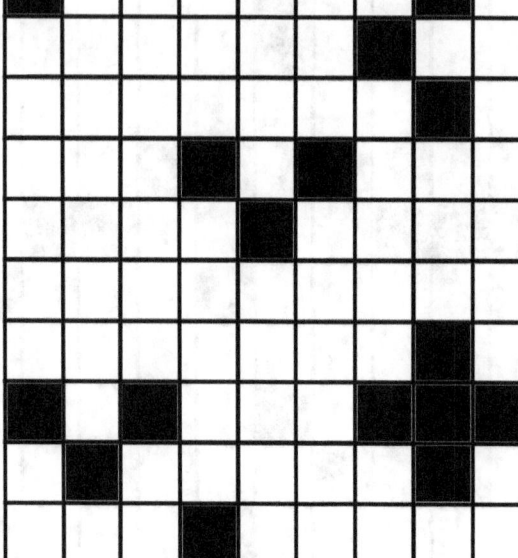

Synge

6 Letter
Bleats
Demand
France
Fresco
Gleams
Hearse
Hot rod
Nicety
Sestet
Snap at
Strays
Tirade

7 Letter
Doublet
Episode
Hateful
Lawsuit
Oration
Outlive
Readopt
Rowdies
Salerno
Serious
Sierras
Tsunami

8 Letter
Bronchus
Day-to-day
Emeritus
Tabouret

11 Letter
Chiaroscuro
Obscurities
See eye to eye
Sovereignty

91

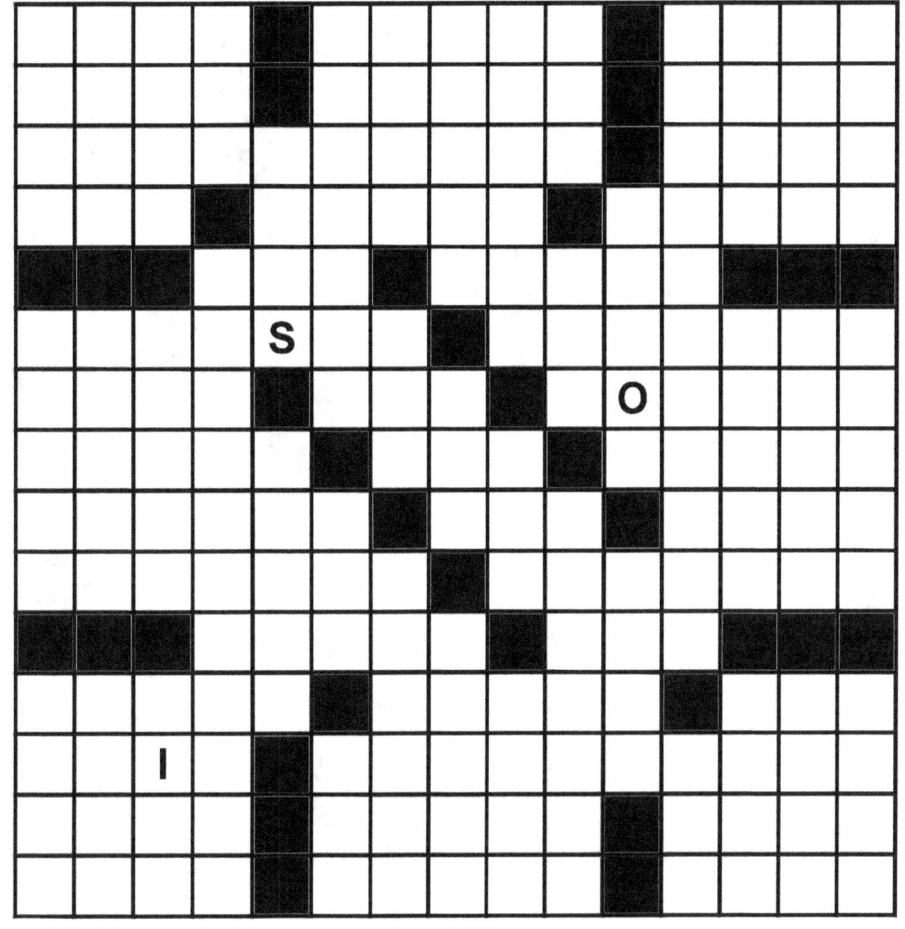

3 Letter
Ate
Gad
Kit
Lac
Lob
Nap
Oft
Pep
Per
Raw
Rev
Sir
Sly
Ten
Web
Woo

4 Letter
A bit
Aide
Coma
Dean
Doff
Edam
Emmy
Gags
Gill
ICAO
Idol
Isis
Lune
Nero
None
Obit
Oily
Omit
Oral
Peed
Rare
Redo
Role
Sine

Stye
Tsar
Upon
Very

5 Letter
Actin
Adore
Aloud
Bialy
Derby
Dross
Dynes
Ebbed
Elbow
Error
Gooey
Guiro
Lisle
Relay

Rhine
Segos
Sidle
Sit-in
Stela
Trace
Yeses
Yikes

6 Letter
Cartel
Ordain
Touchy
Weepie

7 Letter
Bygones
Ego trip
Eyebrow
Niggard
Pyrenes
Transit

10 Letter
Aficionado
Spoonerism

11 Letter
Snout beetle
Undisguised

92

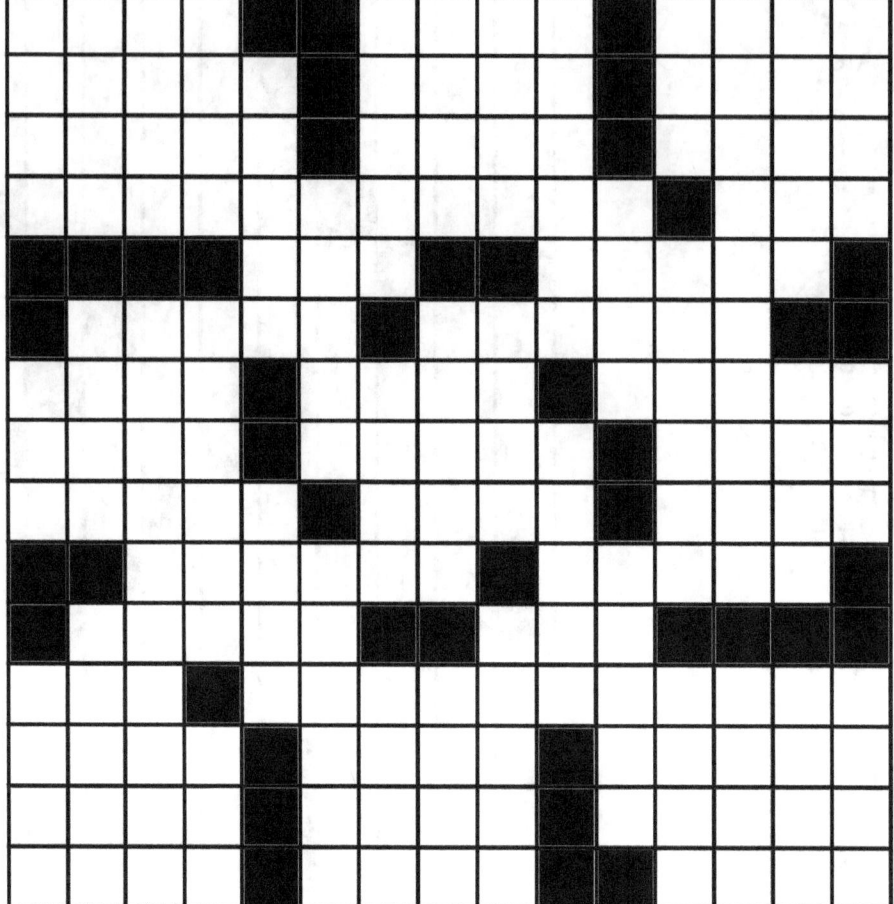

3 Letter
Aye
Eve
Fir
Loy
Pap
Pep
Spa
VII

4 Letter
Arty
Carl
Cool
Ease
Ells
Emus
Feat
Foot
Hoop
Hype
Iota
Isle
Kiwi
Naan
Nets
Noir
Norm
Oboe
Olio
Olla
Oops
Oral
Oreo
Orff
Otto
Piaf
Pish
Prep
Prop
Sage
Same
Sane

Slab
Slub
Snip
Stir
Taut
They
Tows
Unit

5 Letter
Allah
Briar
Broad
Carpi
Easel
Group
Issue
Mirth
Motor
Of age

Pewit
Recap
Rev up
Salal
Stole
Stove
Tying
Verso
Wyatt
Yikes

6 Letter
Abbess
Beside
Isopod
Odessa
Pronto
Repast

10 Letter
Ameliorate
Irrelevant

11 Letter
Effectuates
Pocket knife

93

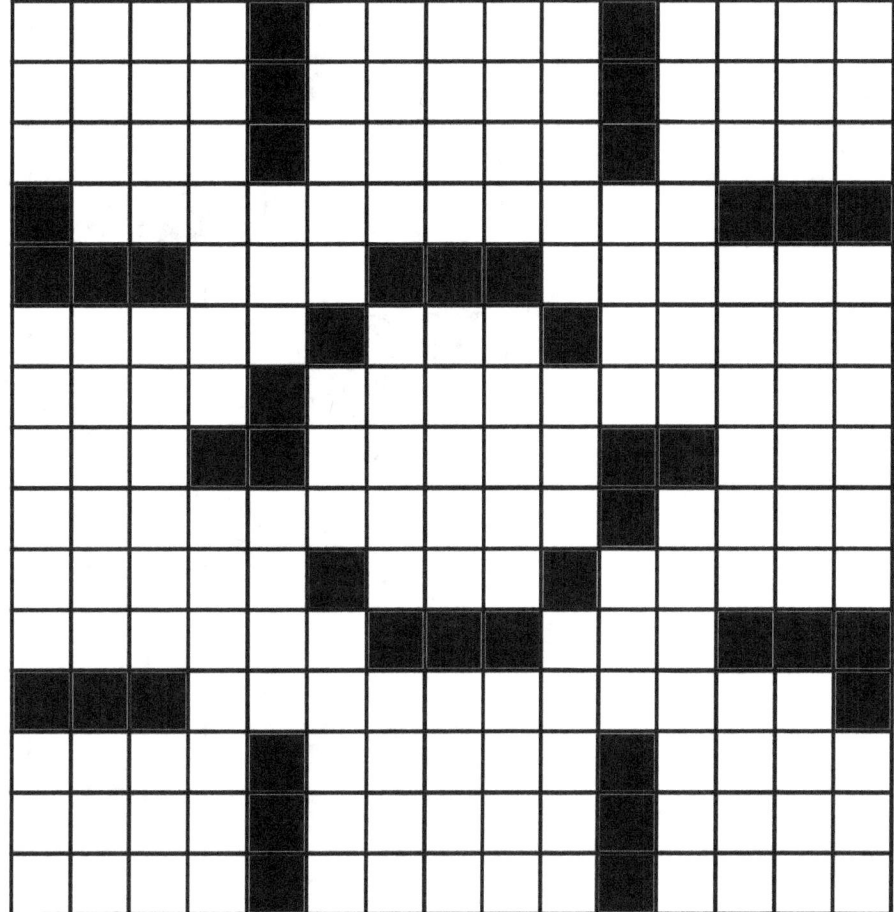

3 Letter
Ala
Ale
Alp
Ana
Cha
Cry
Cue
DNA
Eld
Hrs
Ill
Lac
New
Sop
Tit
Tow
Woo
Yet

4 Letter
Achy
Anis
Area
Aria
Czar
Dele
Emir
Euro
Exam
Gael
Gale
Hart
Heft
Heir
High
Hire
Lest
Lure
Odin
Olio
Oxen
Ring

Sera
Smew
Weir
Zinc

5 Letter
Aerie
Afire
Audio
Cheep
Clasp
Crisp
Derby
Drier
Eagre
Edema
Genii
Grebe
Lemur
Loans

Preps
Radii
Sedge
There

6 Letter
Absorb
Eraser
Halide
Leeway
Neuter
Series
Signal
Thames

7 Letter
Allegro
Omicron
Restart
Sea dogs

10 Letter
Courthouse
Misogynist

11 Letter
Catastrophe
Clearheaded

94

3 Letter
Aah
Ado
Any
Aye
Bro
Eat
Ice
ILO
Ire
Nun
Pen
Pry
Ray
Tug
UFO
VII

4 Letter
Acai
Alee
Arch
Arts
Aver
Bali
Beta
Cain
Defy
Ergo
Fave
Gain
ICAO
Imam
Laud
Mags
Maid
Mali
Mien
Minx
Odor
Ones
Ouch
Rani

RISC
Scot
Song
Year

5 Letter
Abash
Apian
Apnea
Boffo
Clear
Curve
De-ice
Drape
Hades
Letch
Obeah
Ocean
Osier
Renal

Scamp
Sieve
So far
Theta

6 Letter
Anopia
Apercu
Avatar
Dicier
Heroic
Melees
Overdo
Sevens

7 Letter
Immoral
Michael
Moshing
Rolodex

10 Letter
Freebooter
Revivified

11 Letter
Chronometer
Ineluctable

95

3 Letter
Ale
Apt
Eat
Eta
Fro
Gat
Her
ILO
Oca
Psi
Rat
Rpm
Tai
Top

4 Letter
Albs
Baal
Cups
Debs
Film
Omen
Rube
Sego
Serf
Slur
Sumo
Wiry

5 Letter
Adder
Alias
Broom
Emcee
Euros
Fiend
Oaths
Odder
Oomph
Rigor
Salem
Screw
Seats
Steel
Stoep
Swarm
Taser
Toper
Wrote
Yahoo

6 Letter
Sinews
Sirius
Steers
Whirrs

7 Letter
A priori
Beefalo
Cattail
Cordite
Eternal
Hibachi
Orinoco
Yoghurt

8 Letter
Forsooth
Shellacs

9 Letter
Cotter pin
Flag-waver
Pilferers
Referrals
Soldier on
Stowaways
Video game
Windsurfs

96

3 Letter
Ado
Ago
Ape
App
Duo
Erg
Led
Leo
Moo
Oak
Pin
Pod
Rah
San
Sea
Ska
Sol
Tis
Ute
Zap

4 Letter
Amen
Amok
Amos
Atom
Coma
Echt
Efts
Eggs
Gene
Hole
ICBM
Luau
Omit
Or so
Oslo
Pouf
Redo
Ripe
Shag
Silk

VIII
Zeus

5 Letter
Aesop
Ahead
Amino
Apish
Cameo
Cigar
Damns
Embed
Evert
Idiot
Ikons
Ileum
Lemma
Mufti
Pates
Proas

Rhino
Tapir
Tulle
Yoked

6 Letter
Aachen
Ampere
Casbah
Cicero
Facets
Ironic
Retell
Trepan

7 Letter
Appends
Placoid

15 Letter
Higher education
Impenetrability
Loch Ness
monster
Misappropriated

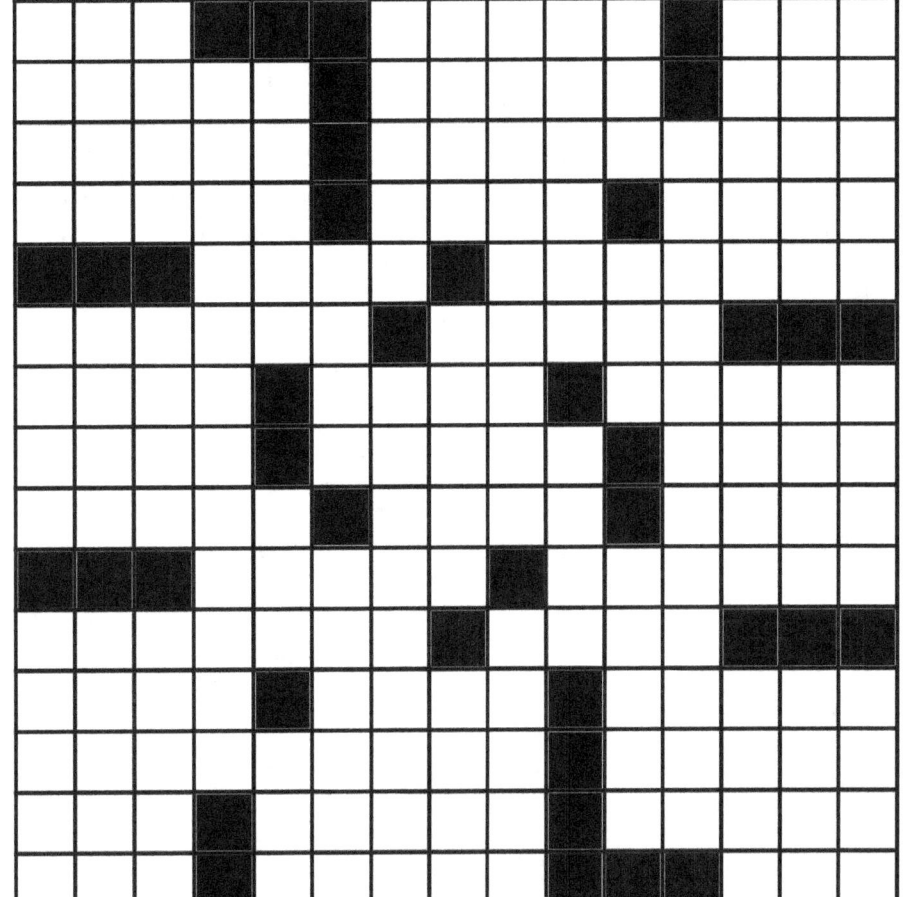

3 Letter
Dis
Ems
Eye
Neo-
Oak
Odd
Ply
Sop
Ult
Yen

4 Letter
Acer
Ache
Ahem
Ammo
Aver
Easy
Else
Etas
Fray
Here
Odor
Olio
Olla
Oman
Omit
Oval
Palp
Pisa
Poor
Raid
Reed
Reps
Roof
Rude
Sank
Stab
Tape
They

5 Letter
A-list
Atoll
Cache
Defog
Doffs
Ether
Ionic
Issue
Koala
Malty
Mikes
Miser
Neath
Nisei
Nonce

Obese
Onion
Pouty
Puppy
Ramie
Rev up
Rodeo
Skate
Stere
Tiara
Ulnae

6 Letter
Entrée
Misfit
Pariah
Taipan

7 Letter
Ladings
Ramekin

9 Letter
Air-intake
Plaintiff
Unalloyed
Volte-face

12 Letter
Self-interest
Trick or treat

98

3 Letter
Act
Awe
Dud
E'er
Eld
Ere
FDA
Mas
Obi
Rad
Rho
Sea
Sly
Son
TNT
Via

4 Letter
A few
Aden
Into
Isis
Noah
Seta
Tall
Tipi
Unit
Yank

5 Letter
Eased
Pants
Sheaf
Tonic

6 Letter
Altair
Assent
Emesis
Fresno
Goiter
Knifes
Leaved
Opiate
Pusses
Ratify
Sea god
Sleuth
Stores
Tonnes

7 Letter
Achenes
Addenda
Arc sine
Bandana
Blow-dry
Cyanide
Dallier
Eddying
Enteron
Eritrea
Intents
Isolate
Lunette
Martini
Ninnies
Oedipal
Purlieu
Tannest
Unitard
Wahines

9 Letter
Eternally
Radiogram

10 Letter
Strike back
Synecdoche

99

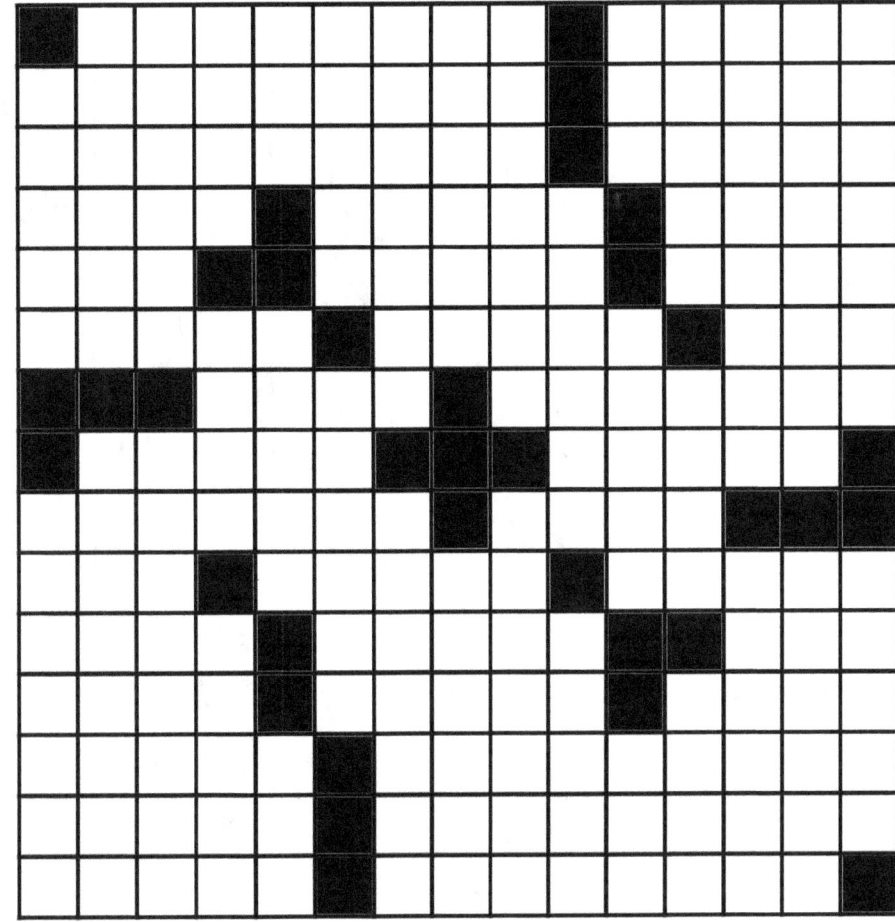

3 Letter
Eon
Ire
Lap
Man
Oct
Tai
TNT
Yin

4 Letter
Acme
Asea
Chew
Erst
Hubs
Into
Item
Meet
Pest
Rime
Seat
Seta

5 Letter
Aural
Cares
Carpi
Floor
Hoagy
Leech
Mercy
Octad
Pasty
Polyp
Recti
Rents
Scuts
Semis
Smash
Snarl
Tansy
Tonne

Trios
Tripe
Utica
Where
Yeast
Yucca

6 Letter
Aisles
Altaic
Bereft
Conned
Estate
Gateau
Greens
On time

7 Letter
Delouse
Distant
Gamiest
Hearers
Phoning
Seaward
Stirs up
Weeping

8 Letter
Apostasy
Edginess
Game show
Hate mail
Triremes
Went into

9 Letter
Attenuate
Paleocene
Sentiment
Unicycles

100

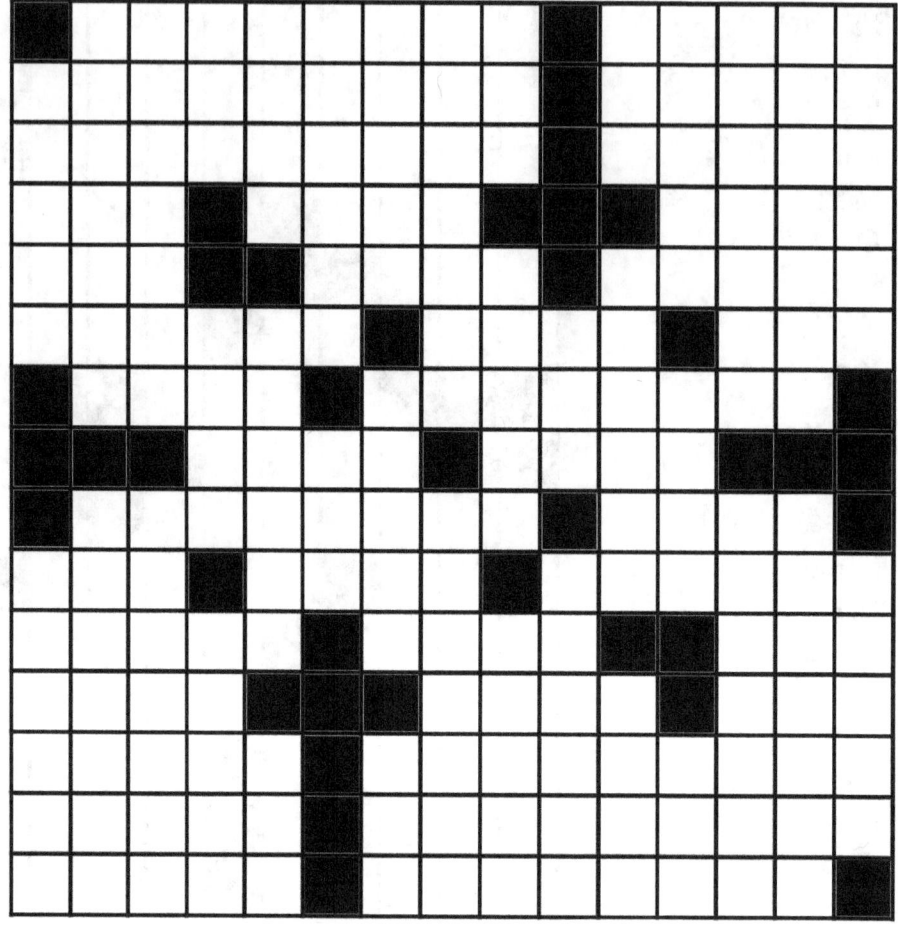

3 Letter
Ala
Asp
Ate
Cop
Cue
Gar
Lao
Min
Opt
She
Ted
Tot
Vas
Zee

4 Letter
Ages
Best
Coal
Crab
Duos
Et al
Etna
Grit
Guar
Lore
NATO
Shoo
Slot
Soda
Taro
Tray

5 Letter
Alibi
Arête
Armor
Aspic
Elide
Firth
Ileum
Marcs
Misdo
Muzak
Nisei
Steep
Stere
Tales
Using
Young

6 Letter
Coupes
Fletch
Kitsch
Smiths
Steams
Thetis
Trivet
Wealth

7 Letter
Attaint
Biotech
Cuestas
Genesis
In-depth
Naughty
Relapse
Reserve
Tie tack

Whatsit

8 Letter
Eye tooth
Gigawatt
Ukuleles
Wrapping

9 Letter
Chevalier
Menagerie
Undreamed
Utterance

101

3 Letter
Ali
Ash
Bro
Cad
Dud
Eft
Eke
Ems
Eye
FAQ
Its
Lat
Nom
Per
Psi
The
Urn
Ute
Vie
Yup

5 Letter
Bronc
Cease
Elite
Elope
Horde
Latte
Loupe
Manna
Owner
Pares
Put in
Raise

6 Letter
Annuli
Damsel
Either
E-mails
Enrage
Estate
Fewest
Lairds
Mayors
Oddest
Quebec
Rename
Salute
Take on
Tousle

Traces

7 Letter
Anemias
Bobcats
Cherubs
Delilah
Demi-sec
Dishrag
Haulage
Heroics
Home run
Nervure
Rampion
Triadic

9 Letter
Rifle shot
Tithe barn

11 Letter
Genetic code
Hyperborean
Replacement
Side streets

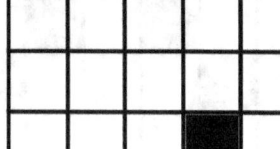

3 Letter
Ate
Bot
Fog
Has
It'd
Nil
Oil
Rib
Set
Tag
Tel
Use

4 Letter
Agar
Boot
Cent
Mega
Mens
Rest
RICO
Slit

5 Letter
Alate
Anele
Green
Grump
Homie
Nasal
Nihil
Onset
Opine
Rials
Sabot

Sauce
Topic
U-boat
Ultra
Utile

6 Letter
Asimov
Awning
Bunion
Cachou
Gaming
Ostler
Pelted
Starer
Tee off

Toasts
Toecap
Uplift

7 Letter
Areolae
Cineast
Defense
Defines
Eats out
Maenads
Nudging
Origami
Psalter
Shut out
Striate

Utensil

9 Letter
Headshots
Piousness

11 Letter
Dielectrics
Nationalist
Reappraises
Toilet water

103

3 Letter
Act
Alp
Big
Cab
Flu
Hes
Hic
Its
Law
Lot
Res
Rid
Sly
Toy
Use
Wit

4 Letter
Anon
Best
Dahl
Elan
Et al
Gyps
Ilia
Inst
Lewd
Mane
Moas
Neap
Nest
Nina
Peen
Pigs
Pupa
Rate
Sped
Tell

5 Letter
Afoot
Indri
Lucre
Paean
Piste
Seats
Snoot
Tacet

6 Letter
Abated
Anises
Banyan
Cavort
Garish
Oh dear
Potash
Useful

7 Letter
Alcalde
Answers
Ideates
Infolds
Lunette
Synergy
Unnoted
Vacancy

9 Letter
Acidified
Ocotillos

11 Letter
Caesar salad
Necessarily
Rhode Island
Uninhibited

104

3 Letter
Air
Ant
Any
Ate
Dot
Edo
Gem
Irk
Kit
Rag
Rib
Sol
Too
Vas
Zig
Zip

4 Letter
Anoa
Aqua
Arco
Arts
Both
Clop
Club
Furl
G-man
Inst
Knit
Memo
Op-ed
Rhea
Ride
RSVP
Seem
Text
That
Ulna

5 Letter
Betel
Croat
Eosin
Lynch
Plane
Steak
Upper
Vapid

6 Letter
Atonic
Dry-rot
Masala
Satiny
Skypes
Tactic
Taipan
Unreel

7 Letter
Adaptor
Get even
Iciness
Pianist
Quietly
Rummage
Tarring
Tipster

9 Letter
Pantaloon
Ptomaines

11 Letter
Chicken feed
Examination
Geopolitics
Ultramarine

105

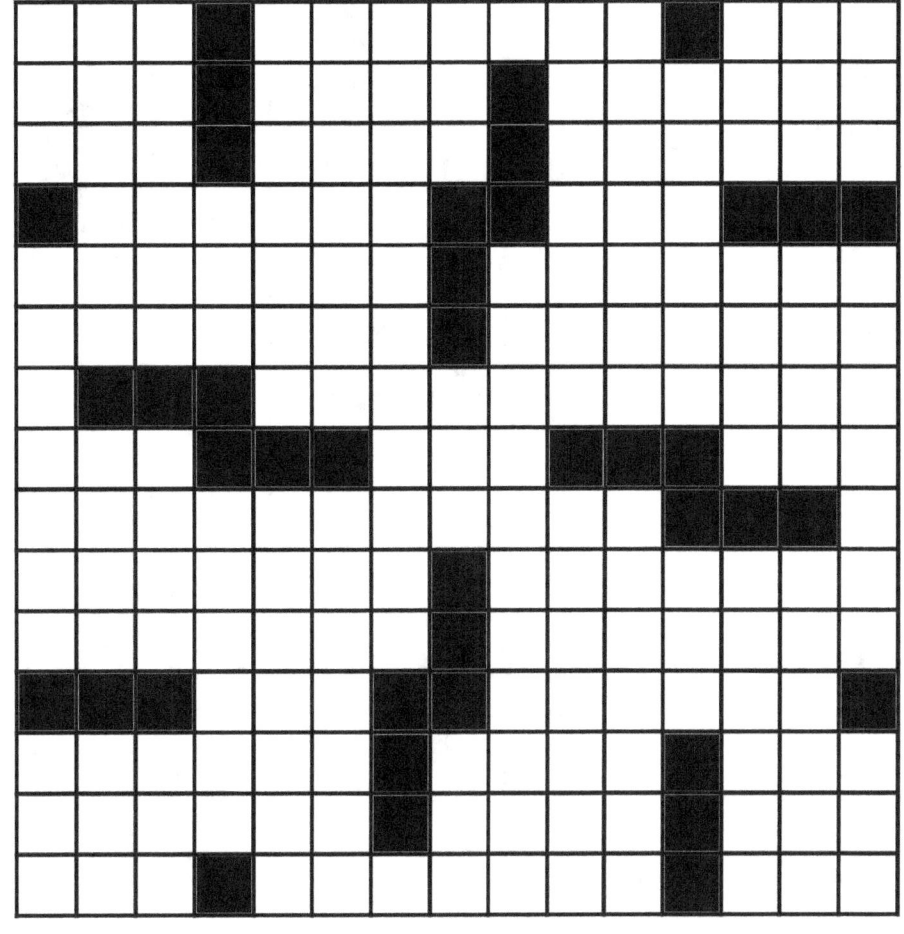

3 Letter
Aah
Ale
Ant
Apr
Apt
Ash
Her
Ira
Its
LAN
Lao
Mat
Mrs
Nth
Pro
Rad
REM
Res
Rip
Tai
Ten
TNT
Ult
Urn
USA
You

4 Letter
Ante
Arch
Gary
In on
Liar
Oahu
Shut
Unco

6 Letter
Adhere
Avatar
Canapé
Etcher
Lean-to
Natron
Neaten
Sat-nav
Scotia
Trepan
Tussle
Utmost

7 Letter
Achaean
Carport
Coal gas
Detests
Indiana
Inherit
Nahuatl
Outrode
Overact
Overate
Overlie
Palmtop
Picasso
Pistols
Revival
Riot gun
Severed
Shuttle
Sponged
Step-ins

11 Letter
Countermine
Grand pianos
Ripsnorting
Strip search

106

107

3 Letter
Ape
Bag
Cos
E'er
Man
Nun
Ova
Rio
Sae
Sea
Tee
Wet

4 Letter
Ammo
Aria
Cube
Esau
Limp
Miso
Moot
Nisi
Orca
Pair
Rear
Sots
Stem
Stet
Tent
Unto

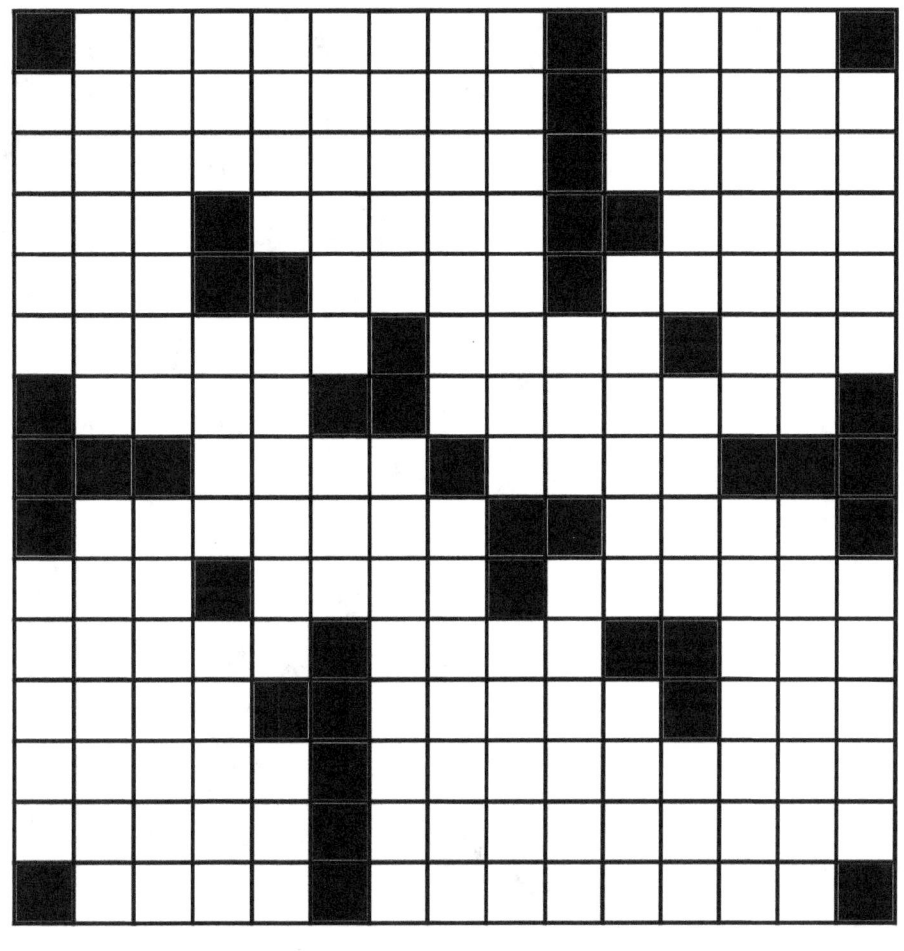

5 Letter
Arose
COBOL
Cocci
Giant
Loots
Nimby
Ollas
Omens
Oxbow
Reuse
Sacra
Satyr
Senna
Sopor
Tinea
Umami

6 Letter
Artist
Lament
Nimbus
No ball
Pathos
Playas

7 Letter
Becomes
Boronic
Caravan
Enrobes
Esteems
Halibut
Myanmar
Origami
Papuans

Relaxes
Rhubarb
Sea bass

8 Letter
Cottages
Ortolans
Scissors
Steamier

9 Letter
Anchorman
Careerist
Nicotiana
Orientate

108

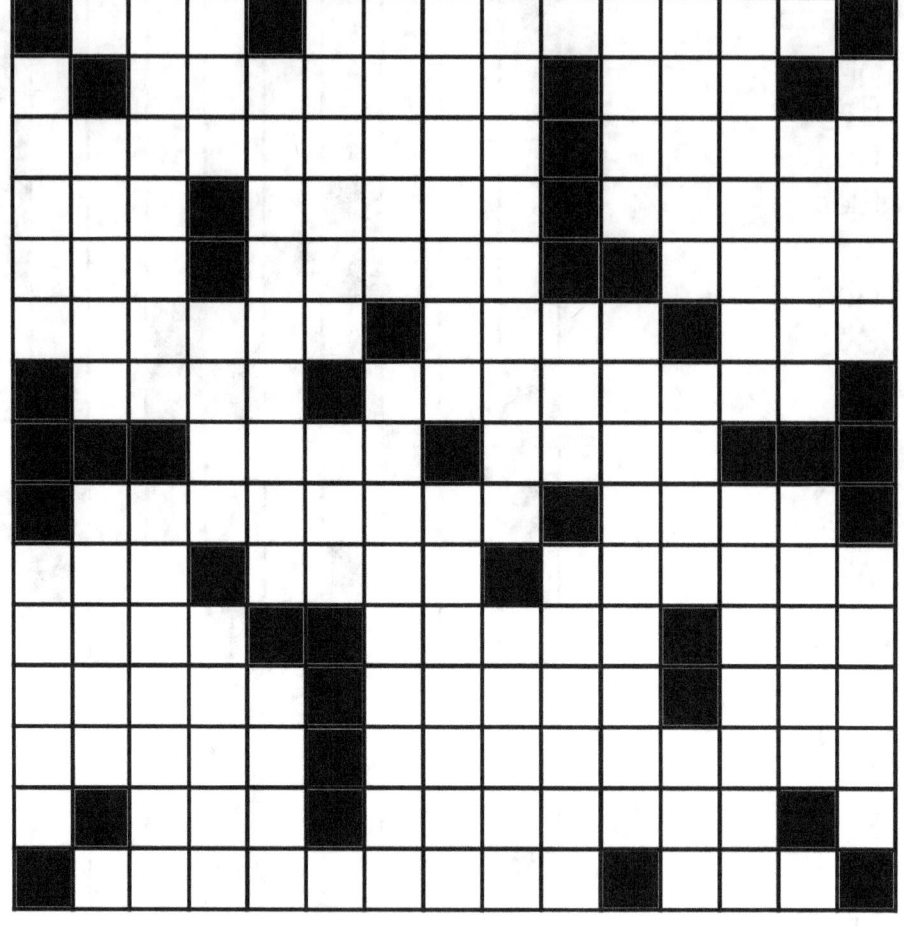

3 Letter
Ago
Alp
Are
Art
Bin
DIY
GNP
Leo
Mao
Moo
Pal
Rim
Set
Yes

4 Letter
Abet
Aces
Aide
Ammo
Boor
Eyed
Grow
Mask
Narc
Poem
Rear
Turn

5 Letter
Amiss
Carve
Egest
Garth
Gigot
Incog
Korea
Lagan
Limen
Loess
Mamas
Maori

Omani
Parka
Slant
Smarm
Starr
Steno
Surge
Toque

6 Letter
Attain
Canary
Carnal
Ski run

7 Letter
Adamant
Eastman
En masse
Entrées
Nepotic
Parvenu
Unequal
Upscale

8 Letter
Dutiable
Survival

9 Letter
Antenatal
Apple tart
Asparagus
Campanile
Developer
Paralysis
Seaworthy
Seclusive

109

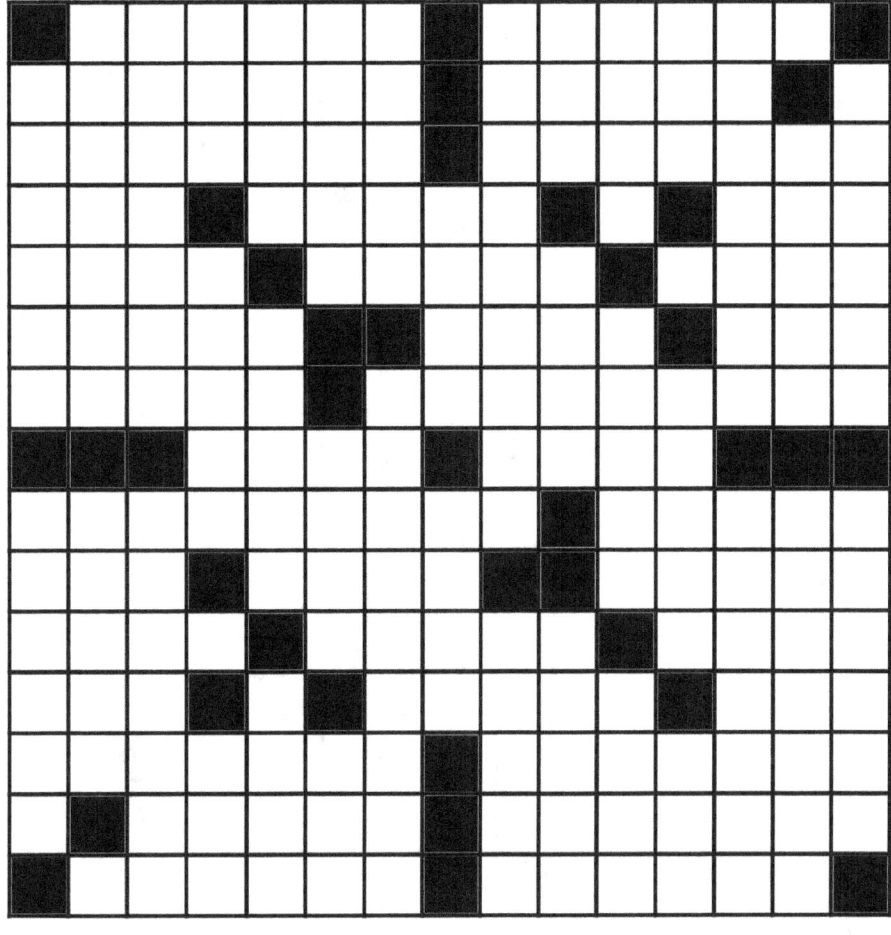

3 Letter
Ale
Dog
Far
Min
Pan
Rag
Row
Tan
URL
Urn
Wee
You

4 Letter
Ally
Byes
Etna
Fino
Ibis
Iraq
Kept
Kohl
Noah
Noll
Ones
Saki
Some
Spot
Tyro
Veil

5 Letter
Colic
Eat on
Greet
Itchy
Karat
Mesas
Myrrh
Negus
Ogees
Pinto
Quest
Samoa
Serve
Sheik
Shelf
Stamp
Stats
Talon
Try-on
Tunic

6 Letter
Bygone
Simoom
Solely
Spuing
Stayer
Strewn
Subdue
Yclept

7 Letter
At heart
Cloacal
Elegist
Encrypt
Hillary
Iron Age
Pioneer
Snowcap
Stirrer

Stringy
Uniform
Unlucky

9 Letter
Pirouette
Plantsman
Steel band
Stuttered

110

3 Letter
Ace
Ale
Alp
Cud
Ilk
Lee
Née
Pan
Tad
Tam
Tee
The
Tho
Ult
Ute
Yah

4 Letter
Boff
Dead
Étui
Floe
ICAO
Loll
NASA
Nips
Prim
Sage
Shmo
Slav

5 Letter
Demon
Doubt
Inept
Manic
Omani
Ovals
Seder
Uh-huh

6 Letter
Accost
Briers
Chorea
Cut-ups
Decamp
Erring
Googol
Insole
Landau
Lanker
Redeem
Rennet
Should
Slogan
Splash
Stay up

7 Letter
Agitate
Amphora
Astound
Beseech
Nahuatl
Naphtha
Palatal
Plicate
Red tide
Reteach
Seducer
Utopian

8 Letter
Cortices
Falconer
Mesoderm
Spatulas

11 Letter
Parallelism
Teetotaller

Solutions

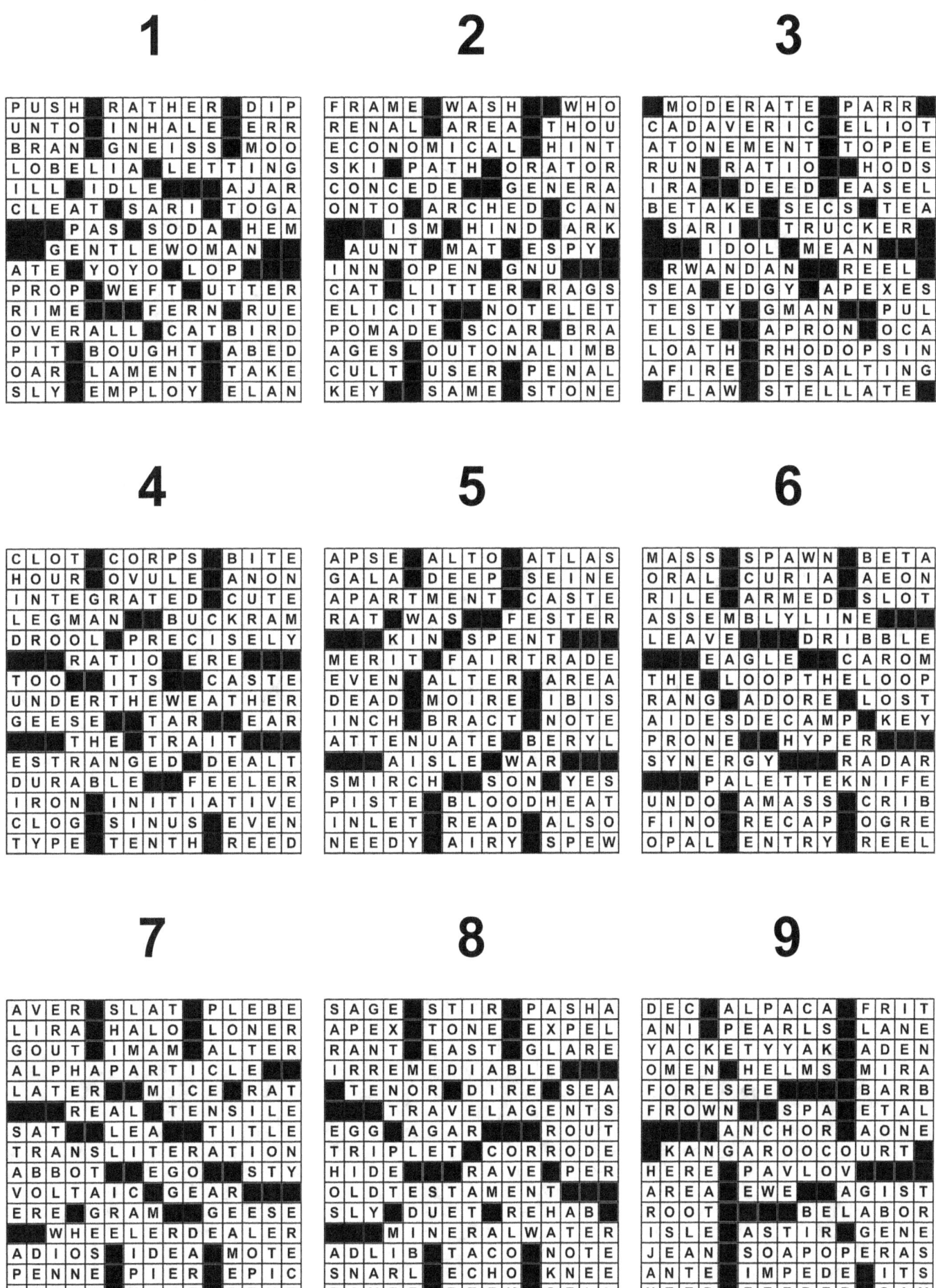

10

```
U N C R O S S ■ D O S ■ F A R
P A R ■ A T T R I B U T I V E
S P O T T E R ■ S E R E N E R
■ H U H ■ E A S T S I D E ■ E
A T T E M P T ■ E E N ■ A L A
T H O S E ■ U R N ■ A C R I D
M A N A G E S ■ D E M O T E S
■ L ■ U ■ O ■ ■ ■ A ■ M ■ D
T E R R I N E ■ T R A P P E R
O N A I R ■ T A R ■ S L A T E
R E M ■ O N E ■ A S P I R E D
P ■ P A N O R A M A ■ E T C
E L A T I O N ■ C R E D I T S
D A R E S S A L A A M ■ T O O
O P T ■ T E L ■ R H U B A R B
```

11

```
D E A F ■ H A L F ■ ■ C O C O
A N T I ■ O R E O ■ I L I A D
R E E X A M I N E ■ C O N G O
E M U ■ R E A D ■ D I C K E R
R A P I E R ■ ■ O U C H ■ ■ ■
■ C A U S E C E L E B R E
E C H O ■ N E T T L E ■ A I L
M O A N ■ ■ C H A ■ ■ A L A S
I L L ■ S T R O V E ■ P I L E
T E L E P R E S E N C E ■ ■
■ B O A T ■ ■ V O X P O P
R E C O U P ■ C O I N ■ A P E
E U R O S ■ A R G O N A U T S
D R A K E ■ G U R U ■ S L I T
O O P S ■ E X E S ■ P I C S
```

12

```
E T A L ■ R O O T ■ ■ R O P E
B A N E ■ E C H O ■ R E R U N
B R O A D J U M P ■ E V E R T
S P A N I E L S ■ U N E A S E
■ ■ ■ O C A ■ I N O R D E R
R A P I D T R A N S I T ■ ■
O L I V E ■ S T A R ■ T W O
A L K Y ■ D E C O Y ■ L A I D
D Y E ■ C I A O ■ V E R N E
■ H E A R T S T R I N G S ■
R E L E A R N ■ M O O ■ ■ ■
U N E A S Y ■ B A R O N E S S
S U A V E ■ D A R T M O U T H
E R R E D ■ A C M E ■ O R E O
S E N D ■ W H Y S ■ N O P E
```

13

```
C R O P ■ A S K S ■ A S T I R
L A V A ■ U T A H ■ L I A N A
A J A R ■ R A V E ■ P R O N G
W A L K I E T A L K I E ■ ■
■ ■ A D O S ■ F U N ■ E R A
■ E A S E L ■ ■ R E L I E F
T A N ■ S E C O N D S I G H T
U R G E ■ O R B ■ T H E E
F L I G H T D E C K S ■ T A R
T A N G O S ■ ■ E I G H T ■
S P A ■ A A H ■ L Y R A
■ I R R E V E R S I B L E
B L O O D ■ L E V I ■ E R I N
R O U T E ■ O D I N ■ T I E D
A T T A R ■ T A N G ■ Y O U S
```

14

```
G R A B ■ M A T ■ ■ A L I B I
L I R A ■ E G I S ■ P E R I L
U S S R ■ N O G O ■ S W A N K
T H O R O U G H B R E D S ■ ■
S I N E W ■ ■ T E E ■ ■ C I A
■ N E R V E R A C K I N G
R E G ■ E E N ■ P U E B L O
A M O N G S T ■ Z I E G L E R
G A L O O T ■ P E N ■ ■ E T A
G I F T O F T H E G A B ■ ■
A L L ■ U S E ■ F A T S O
■ I M P L A N T A T I O N S
P A N E L ■ R O A R ■ L A I C
A N K L E ■ S L I M ■ E D D A
P A S T A ■ S L Y ■ D Y E R
```

15

```
■ S P A W N ■ ■ S L U B S
P L A T O O N ■ S T E P I N S
R E S T A T E ■ T E N S P O T
I N S I D E R ■ R E S T O R E
E D A M ■ V I O L ■ A L E E
S E D E R ■ E S P Y ■ T A R P
R O S I N ■ T H A L E R S
■ ■ N O W H E R E ■ ■ ■
■ P R O G R A M ■ D E A T H
T R A P ■ T R U E ■ S T A I R
R O V E ■ H I S S ■ A N T E
O V E R A W E ■ T O C C A T A
M E N A G E S ■ E N R A G E D
P R E T E S T ■ R E A M E R S
■ B R E S T ■ ■ S P A R S
```

16

```
■ P O L ■ T R A I P S I N G
A ■ M A H O U T S ■ W O O ■ E
B R I C A B R A C ■ O W N E R
E E N ■ L O A T H ■ B A Z A R
T A O ■ F O L I A ■ N E V E
S C U L P T ■ M E N U ■ R E D
■ T S A R ■ M E M E N T O S
■ ■ V I S A ■ I T C H ■ ■
■ M E A C U L P A ■ O A S T
M A X ■ E M I R ■ S N I P E S
U S P S ■ ■ C O M I C ■ A N I
M A U L S ■ A L O N E ■ N E B
P I N U P ■ C O N G R U I T Y
S ■ G N U ■ I N T E N S E ■ L
■ B E G R U D G E S ■ E L K
```

17

```
■ S T E A D ■ ■ R A G S ■
S T E N C I L ■ O P E N A I R
M A R T I N I ■ B A P T I S E
A B R I D G E ■ S P L I N T S
S L I T ■ ■ T R Y ■ F E E
H E E L S ■ A C A I ■ U R N
■ D R E A D L O C K S ■ L S D
■ ■ F I B U L A E ■ ■
A D S ■ E V A N E S C E N T
B E Y ■ A C T S ■ T R E W S
R E S ■ E G O ■ ■ E R I E
U P T O P A R ■ A B I L E N E
P R O M O T E ■ L O C O I S M
T E L E X E S ■ B L O N D E S
■ D E N Y ■ ■ A N G S T ■
```

18

```
■ C U B I C ■ ■ D I C E R ■
T O R E R O S ■ C E R U M E N
E P I G O N E ■ A V A R I C E
S Y N O N Y M ■ R E N E G E R
L I A R ■ ■ I D O L ■ A R I D
A N T R A ■ S I L O ■ L E V Y
■ G E A R S ■ R E P U L S E
■ ■ M E A N D E R ■ ■
■ M A N S A R D ■ R E B E L
T O G A ■ P O L O ■ A U G U R
A T O M ■ L I S T ■ ■ L O N E
L I N E M A N ■ H A B I T E D
E V I D E N T ■ E R E M I T E
S E S A M E S ■ R E S I S T S
■ S T Y E S ■ ■ S T A T E ■
```

19

20

21

22

23

24

25

26

27

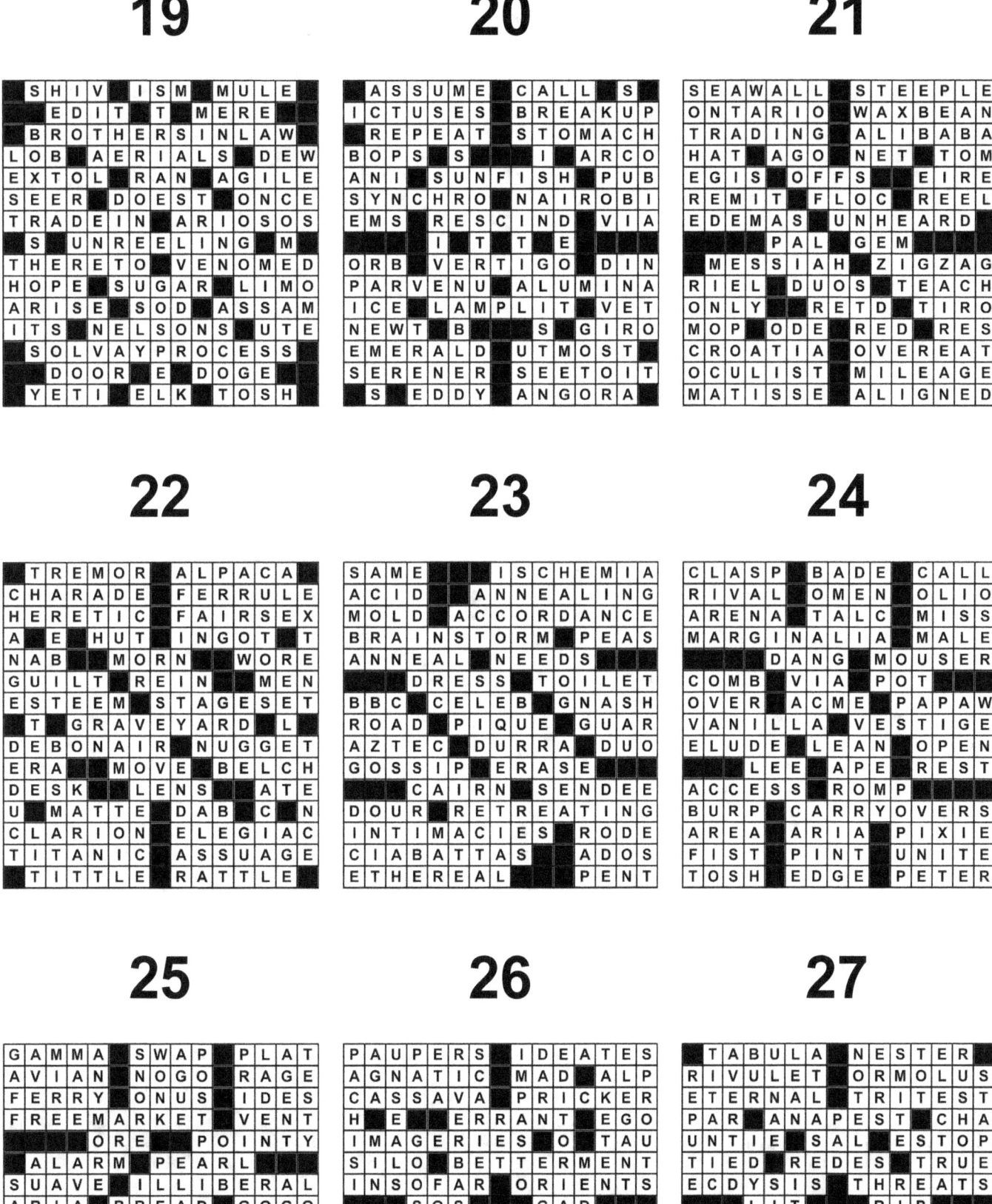

28

```
  PATE    ICECAP
GARROTE  CARAVAN
ALMONER  EREMITE
LARD  ERECT  PARA
ODE    AGO    TIT
RISC  KNOLL  BOO
ENTRANT  DIVERT
    USE    VAT
 HEEHAW  VINEGAR
 ANT  DRYAD  LAZE
RIG    EEL    SIP
ORAL  OASIS  MEMO
ACROBAT  SERIOUS
MUDBATH  EXECUTE
 TEETHE  DASH
```

29

```
 MUSES   COCAS
 NOMENCLATURES
RAMPAGE  STREAKY
ISM MONOCOT  LYE
PAYDIRT  AMASSES
   ALGEBRAIC
MISDEED  ANNOYER
AREA       ROLE
TAXICAB  ATRIUMS
   SEBORRHEA
ORATRIX  ORDEALS
FOP ALIQUOT  ZIP
FORAMEN  SMARTLY
 FILINGCABINET
 LACES   LILAC
```

30

```
EGO  METE   BRIMS
KID  ADEN  MOOLAH
ENDANGER   IODINE
   WAYSANDMEANS
NOIR     GAS
ARMY   STENTORIAN
RIP  WOOS   NUBIA
ROAMING   FILBERT
OLLAS   LACY   RET
WEATHEREYE  SIRE
       CON   USSR
ACHILLESHEEL
CHOREA   MONIKERS
RAREST  EMIR   AYE
ERNST    NODE  REX
```

31

```
DOTE  EDAM   SHALE
OVER  NAGA   PUREE
LEER  DRAG   INCUR
ENDANGERMENT
   NEAR  AGO   PHI
 MODEM     OUTSET
LAV DEMONSTRATE
AREA   ILO    YLEM
DIRTYOLDMAN   MRS
ENDEAR      VERSO
NEO  WEE   PESO
   UNSCIENTIFIC
OKAPI   LONG   LADE
PINON   ANNE   EVER
STING   TSAR   DEAN
```

32

```
AWN  SOT   SCRIBE
LEO  THOU  LOANER
ITS  AMEN  APICES
SLYLY   COVENANT
TYPE  SWEDEN
 AUSTERE   HICKS
BAR  PYRE   ACARI
ANKLE  EMU  GELID
SNEER  ONCE   USE
HAREM  ANTONYM
    AMNION  ANON
STACCATO   AMITY
CAREEN  UNIX  AHA
AMENTS  SARI  TEL
BESTIE   YES   ERA
```

33

```
ALSO  COSTA   CITE
MENU  RAPID   ROAD
INON  ATEAM   UNTO
CIRCUMSCRIBE
ENTER    ATALOSS
    SINGE    BERNE
SOT  COUNTRYSEAT
ONES  RADIO   TAFT
DISCOMMODES   DUO
OCTAL   WESTS
MEALIES     ALTAR
   POLLINGBOOTH
DELI  BONEY   UPTO
VAIN  OTTER   GEAN
DREG  WHORE   HERE
```

34

```
ORACLES  VOMITUS
BUG  ORIFICE  USA
SMOKING  SCENTED
C N TEN  CID  T I
UNITE  AMIDSHIPS
RAZORBLADE  ONIT
EVENER  R  NUDGES
 A  RAW  OTT  R
THRESH  A  ATTICA
ROOT  MIDDLEAGES
ASIAMINOR  RINSE
C S ANC ATM  O P
ESTONIA  PHOEBES
ROE  ISSUERS  LEI
SURNAME  SUTLERS
```

35

```
UGLI   DATA   CASTE
SEAR   EWER   ULCER
UNDO   TARE   BLEAR
REINCARNATION
ERE   RID   ATTACK
RASCAL  AND   ROE
   OVERDO   FAIRY
 CANADIANBACON
FACET   SPEECH
EVE   ACT   SIESTA
WARMER  POL   TOT
 BANKSTATEMENT
EVICT   LAST   APSE
LITHE   ELSE   SPIN
MAYOR   DEED   HELD
```

36

```
SUMAC   RISC   REST
EVERY   ONTO   ICAO
TELIC   ATOM   GLUT
SADDLESOAP   HATE
     OTT   RUTTED
 FRANC   HAIFA
PLEBE   POISONGAS
AONE   EAGRE   GURU
SWORDPLAY   SLAIN
    RISEN   OPERA
SALAMI     ADO
TWAT   LUMBERJACK
ANTI   OREO   RANEE
VETO   NEAR   APING
EDEN   SALT   NESTS
```

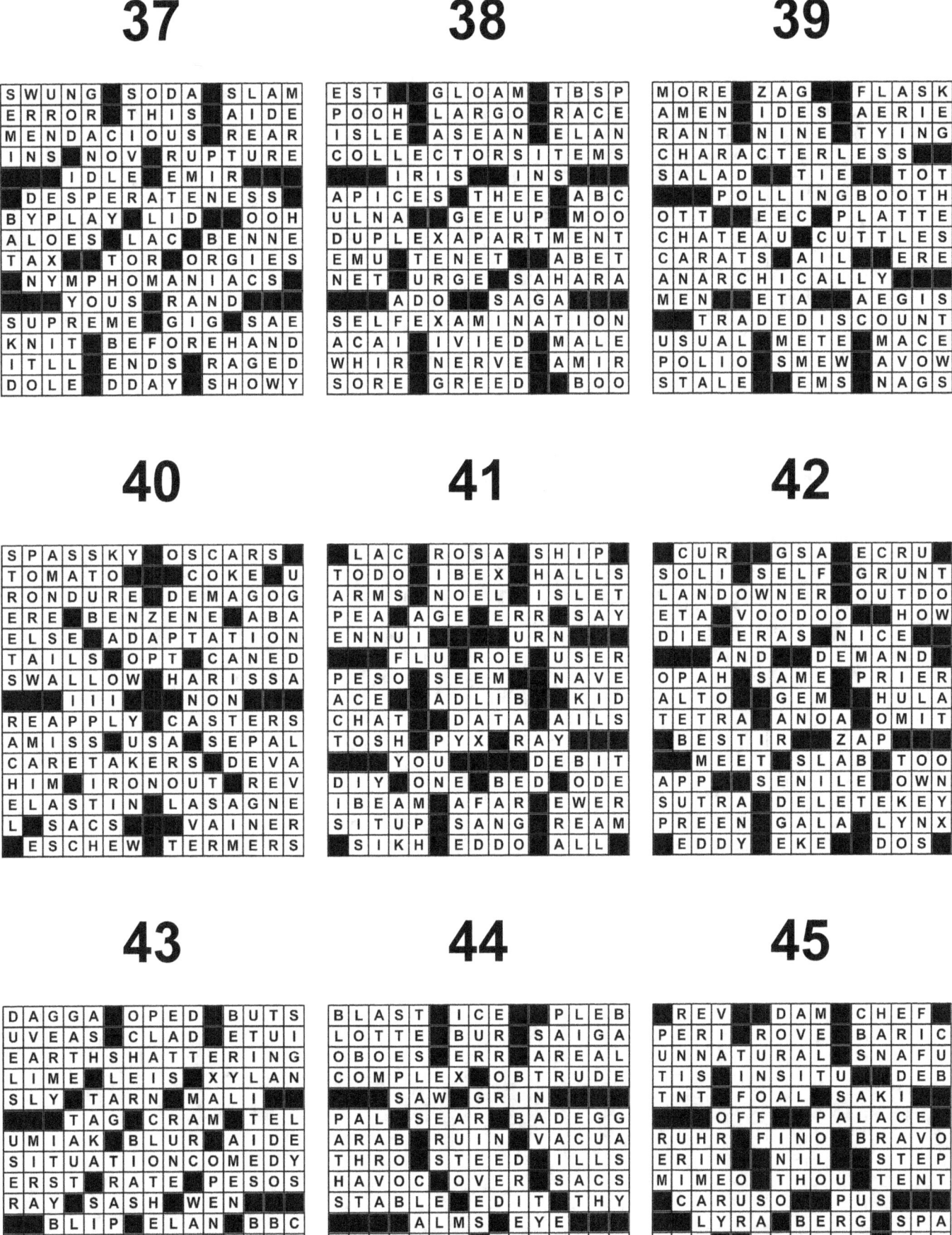

46

```
KAY . OPAH . GOGO .
ROLE . KIWI . EBONY
IRIS . REEF . CIRCA
SEE . LAD . ILK . YEW
CANOE . . . ION .
. . PAS . AGE . URGE
TACT . KOLA . BERG
AVE . INPUT . POI
CODA . THRU . ASKS
OWED . MOA . GUT .
. OVA . . SETIN
DDT . ADD . BOA . ONE
ORIEL . HOOK . BABA
METRO . ANOA . ODOR
. GOER . LORY . PYX .
```

47

```
SHED . SCHOOLMATE
TUNE . POORHOUSES
OMEN . ANTIBODIES
MIMICS . LEON . ANA
ADIEU . WILY . STAY
COERCIONS . BEIGE
HRS . KOOK . BRACER
. JOWL . MAIM .
MACULA . BONG . POT
UPEND . PURGATIVE
SHMO . VISE . NAMER
LOB . RICH . IDLERS
INAMORATAS . KNEE
MILITARISM . ETAL
SAILCLOTHS . DOTY
```

48

```
ARP . GULF . SOREST
BOA . OREO . ERASER
OAR . TSAR . TITTLE
DDT . OUSE . TOTALS
EMIT . LEI . ELATES
SATORI . GREENERY
. PAGANINI .
. SAFEDEPOSIT
. EXECUTOR
AMNESIAC . TEETER
LOOSED . HUE . MATE
PASCAL . ASTI . LIP
INHUME . NUTS . IRE
NEEDER . GAEL . TEL
ERRORS . ELSE . YES
```

49

```
DUAL . GAB . SLOTH
ELBE . OKRA . AERIE
ANON . BIOS . MODEM
LAUGHINGHYENA .
SETTO . LEO . IRE
. HERRINGBONES
SAL . EYE . HAREMS
PROPANE . CUMBRIA
EGOIST . OUR . STY
LUNCHEONETTE .
LEY . RUG . ANIMA
. BEASTOFBURDEN
CHILL . DIAL . ALTO
RINSE . ONTO . GEED
YESES . GET . ERSE
```

50

```
PRONTO . RIOTS .
REFER . A . SPOKES
COFFEE . CASEWORK
ATE . MURMUR . PRY
TERATOGENIC . JOB
CARRELL . INUTERO
H . ANNOY . OGLE . X
. SLIT . . ANEW
X . CELL . SATUP . A
MALARIA . EMERIES
AGE . HOTHEADEDLY
SEA . ONIONS . EVE
ENDTOEND . SUBMIT
STEAKS . S . ETUIS
. RUSSO . TRENCH
```

51

```
HIST . TAMIL . EMIT
ADAR . AMINO . TARO
LILY . CALLA . CYAN
MOVIETHEATRE .
AMONG . . WHATSIT
. GIROS . PENNE
FOB . SUBCONTRACT
OTIS . LOUPE . AFAR
SHOPKEEPERS . USA
SEMEN . SNOOP .
ERELONG . FITIN
. TWILIGHTZONE
OSLO . TIBIA . ZIGS
LIEU . EDIFY . ALOT
DRAT . RESTS . SETS
```

52

```
SISAL . PHONE . RIB
ADAGE . IOTAS . EDO
PERIPATETIC . EER
SAINTLY . OARSMAN
. GAP . DOABLE
OFFS . AGES . WHO
PER . CIVIC . IDLE
ETAS . ARENA . BIER
DANA . SONAR . EGG
. CPA . STIR . ADOS
ATHOME . OLD .
HAIRNET . STAMINA
ENS . IRONPYRITES
AGE . OILER . CREAK
DOE . NEEDY . HEMPS
```

53

```
FAR . SORE . RUINER
APE . AVID . IGNORE
TIC . REND . PASTED
WETTINGAGENT .
ACAI . . UNDERGO
SELLS . GSA . APIAN
. DIALING . CGI
OBSERVATIONPOST
POE . EMANATE .
ESTER . ORE . HEROD
CHATEAU . VALE
. HAIRPINBENDS
PRYERS . OBOE . CHI
SPINEL . RIVE . HAS
IMPEDE . TSAR . OTT
```

54

```
. SITUS . ALE . ANT
POULENC . HAS . DOE
EYELASH . ANTLION
LED . MOOS . DRIEST
TREF . LOT . FUGUES
. LADLE . ASH
OFFAL . BAAL . TOLU
PLATINUMBLONDES
TUTU . USSR . LIEGE
. LEI . HAYDN
ASPENS . IDO . GUSH
DUENNA . PAGE . NEO
OROTUND . NUMERAL
PAN . ICY . TRINITY
THY . SEE . STREP .
```

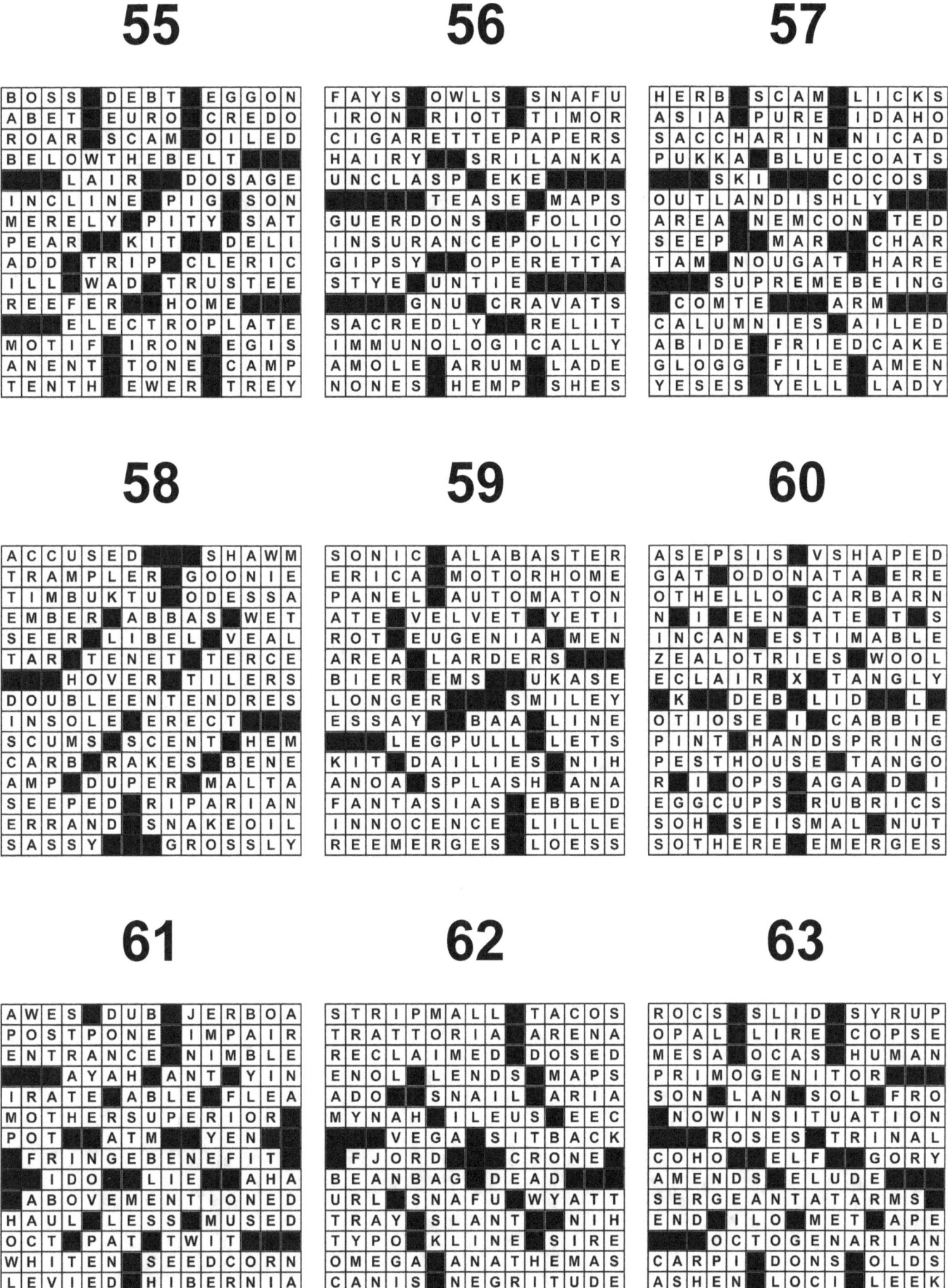

55

```
B O S S ■ D E B T ■ E G G O N
A B E T ■ E U R O ■ C R E D O
R O A R ■ S C A M ■ O I L E D
B E L O W T H E B E L T ■ ■ ■
■ ■ ■ L A I R ■ ■ D O S A G E
I N C L I N E ■ P I G ■ S O N
M E R E L Y ■ P I T Y ■ S A T
P E A R ■ K I T ■ ■ D E L I
A D D ■ T R I P ■ C L E R I C
I L L ■ W A D ■ T R U S T E E
R E E F E R ■ ■ H O M E ■ ■ ■
■ ■ ■ E L E C T R O P L A T E
M O T I F ■ I R O N ■ E G I S
A N E N T ■ T O N E ■ C A M P
T E N T H ■ E W E R ■ T R E Y
```

56

```
F A Y S ■ O W L S ■ S N A F U
I R O N ■ R I O T ■ T I M O R
C I G A R E T T E P A P E R S
H A I R Y ■ ■ S R I L A N K A
U N C L A S P ■ E K E ■ ■ ■
■ ■ ■ T E A S E ■ M A P S
G U E R D O N S ■ F O L I O
I N S U R A N C E P O L I C Y
G I P S Y ■ ■ O P E R E T T A
S T Y E ■ U N T I E ■ ■ ■
■ ■ G N U ■ C R A V A T S
S A C R E D L Y ■ R E L I T
I M M U N O L O G I C A L L Y
A M O L E ■ A R U M ■ L A D E
N O N E S ■ H E M P ■ S H E S
```

57

```
H E R B ■ S C A M ■ L I C K S
A S I A ■ P U R E ■ I D A H O
S A C C H A R I N ■ N I C A D
P U K K A ■ B L U E C O A T S
■ ■ ■ S K I ■ ■ C O C O S
O U T L A N D I S H L Y ■ ■
A R E A ■ N E M C O N ■ T E D
S E E P ■ M A R ■ ■ C H A R
T A M ■ N O U G A T ■ H A R E
■ ■ S U P R E M E B E I N G
■ C O M T E ■ ■ A R M ■ ■ ■
C A L U M N I E S ■ A I L E D
A B I D E ■ F R I E D C A K E
G L O G G ■ F I L E ■ A M E N
Y E S E S ■ Y E L L ■ L A D Y
```

58

```
A C C U S E D ■ ■ S H A W M
T R A M P L E R ■ G O O N I E
T I M B U K T U ■ O D E S S A
E M B E R ■ A B B A S ■ W E T
S E E R ■ L I B E L ■ V E A L
T A R ■ T E N E T ■ T E R C E
■ ■ H O V E R ■ T I L E R S
D O U B L E E N T E N D R E S
I N S O L E ■ E R E C T ■ ■
S C U M S ■ S C E N T ■ H E M
C A R B ■ R A K E S ■ B E N E
A M P ■ D U P E R ■ M A L T A
S E E P E D ■ R I P A R I A N
E R R A N D ■ S N A K E O I L
S A S S Y ■ ■ G R O S S L Y
```

59

```
S O N I C ■ A L A B A S T E R
E R I C A ■ M O T O R H O M E
P A N E L ■ A U T O M A T O N
A T E ■ V E L V E T ■ Y E T I
R O T ■ E U G E N I A ■ M E N
A R E A ■ L A R D E R S ■ ■
B I E R ■ E M S ■ U K A S E
L O N G E R ■ ■ S M I L E Y
E S S A Y ■ B A A ■ L I N E
■ ■ L E G P U L L ■ L E T S
K I T ■ D A I L I E S ■ N I H
A N O A ■ S P L A S H ■ A N A
F A N T A S I A S ■ E B B E D
I N N O C E N C E ■ L I L L E
R E E M E R G E S ■ L O E S S
```

60

```
A S E P S I S ■ V S H A P E D
G A T ■ O D O N A T A ■ E R E
O T H E L L O ■ C A R B A R N
N ■ I ■ E E N ■ A T E ■ T ■ S
I N C A N ■ E S T I M A B L E
Z E A L O T R I E S ■ W O O L
E C L A I R ■ X ■ T A N G L Y
■ K ■ D E B ■ L I D ■ ■ L ■
O T I O S E ■ I ■ C A B B I E
P I N T ■ H A N D S P R I N G
P E S T H O U S E ■ T A N G O
R ■ I ■ O P S ■ A G A ■ D ■ I
E G G C U P S ■ R U B R I C S
S O H ■ S E I S M A L ■ N U T
S O T H E R E ■ E M E R G E S
```

61

```
A W E S ■ D U B ■ J E R B O A
P O S T P O N E ■ I M P A I R
E N T R A N C E ■ N I M B L E
■ ■ A Y A H ■ A N T ■ Y I N
I R A T E ■ A B L E ■ F L E A
M O T H E R S U P E R I O R ■
P O T ■ ■ A T M ■ ■ Y E N ■
■ F R I N G E B E N E F I T ■
■ ■ I D O ■ L I E ■ ■ A H A
■ A B O V E M E N T I O N E D
H A U L ■ L E S S ■ M U S E D
O C T ■ P A T ■ T W I T ■ ■
W H I T E N ■ S E E D C O R N
L E V I E D ■ H I B E R N I A
S N E E R S ■ E N S ■ Y E G G
```

62

```
S T R I P M A L L ■ T A C O S
T R A T T O R I A ■ A R E N A
R E C L A I M E D ■ D O S E D
E N O L ■ L E N D S ■ M A P S
A D O ■ S N A I L ■ A R I A
M Y N A H ■ I L E U S ■ E E C
■ ■ V E G A ■ S I T B A C K
■ F J O R D ■ ■ C R O N E ■
B E A N B A G ■ D E A D ■ ■
U R L ■ S N A F U ■ W Y A T T
T R A Y ■ S L A N T ■ N I H
T Y P O ■ K L I N E ■ S I R E
O M E G A ■ A N A T H E M A S
C A N I S ■ N E G R I T U D E
K N O C K ■ T R E A T I S E S
```

63

```
R O C S ■ S L I D ■ S Y R U P
O P A L ■ L I R E ■ C O P S E
M E S A ■ O C A S ■ H U M A N
P R I M O G E N I T O R ■ ■
S O N ■ L A N ■ S O L ■ F R O
■ N O W I N S I T U A T I O N
■ ■ R O S E S ■ T R I N A L
C O H O ■ ■ E L F ■ ■ G O R Y
A M E N D S ■ E L U D E ■ ■
S E R G E A N T A T A R M S
E N D ■ I L O ■ M E T ■ A P E
■ ■ O C T O G E N A R I A N
C A R P I ■ D O N S ■ O L D S
A S H E N ■ L O C I ■ L E E K
T H O N G ■ E N O L ■ E D D Y
```

64

```
 BEHEST  SPIRIT
VANUATU CETACEA
ANTHRAX REAPERS
MAR  REFILL BEL
PLASHED PSI ONE
ELITE OUT APACE
DYNAST S INSTEP
   I OPART E
REDRAW G SPUING
OBESE LEA UDDER
SOS OCA GENOESE
ENS NORMAN  ATE
TIERING RELATED
SERIATE IMAGERY
 STONES CYCADS
```

65

```
COGNAC  SHASTA
APRICOT GHERKIN
REALTOR ROAMING
ART SEAFOOD PHI
TAEL ECLAT UPON
STROP KIN OPERA
 ESTER P STERN
  TEAM JOHN
 CHEVY D LEDGE
SHARE SOS RELAX
TORY CLOTH DORM
ROD PHARAOH RNA
ASPIRIN ROOKIES
NEARING RELEASE
 DYNAMO  YEASTS
```

66

```
 SEW  WEB  OPED
ACME CAME DOYEN
FACESAVER EDEMA
ARE CLERGY  SOY
RYE AIRY OATH
  IMP  MUTUAL
SPAN HIDE ENDOW
ALMS  ROE  NOVA
CUBIC INTO EWER
 SITUPS  ILL
 GURU PALE ADD
EMU NUANCE LEI
BOOTS REGARDING
BRUIT EARN IBIS
 ESPY ANY  DIM
```

67

```
REFS  EDEMA MOSH
IDLE WOTAN ARCO
BEEN ENACT REAL
 NATURALHISTORY
  INST ICKY
BYTES ENS IRATE
EARNER IMP GOV
CHATTELMORTGAGE
KOI FOB YEOMAN
SOTHO AYE LEAST
 OWED LEIS
ROCKETLAUNCHER
UGLI HINDU OKAY
TRUE INNER MEGA
SEER CEASE EDAM
```

68

```
SCAM SPAS PAILS
HALO OAHU OLDIE
ACKNOWLEDGEMENT
FAITH MOUSSAKA
TOEHOLD KAY
 OAKUM HERA
NOISETTE COSEC
INTHESAMEBREATH
PECAN PROTRUDE
ASHY OUTGO
 PAN OTTOMAN
ISOLATED ALONE
MALECHAUVINISTS
AGIST SLIT VERT
MOOTS ELMS EYES
```

69

```
TETANIC YUK DEN
ELECTROPOSITIVE
PARTHENOGENESIS
ITS GSA SAILS
DEEP BOY FERN
 ALES TRY FAY
ANALOG FOE ERE
LAC POLEMIC CIA
SAC NEW GUITAR
ONO III SHED
 ULNA TNT SWOB
ICTUS BAA HUE
FERTILECRESCENT
FREEDOMOFSPEECH
YES ETA STAPLES
```

70

```
VOCATIVES RIGS
ABOMINATES ANOA
PERPETRATE TSAR
OLD DREG ALKALI
RISC USER EAT
 LASERS ONICE
PEDANT EVE GAUD
AVERTED PUPATED
NISI DID LAREDO
GLENN GIGOLO
 LEI SONG OFFS
BEETLE ROIL LEA
ASCI REASSUMING
WATS REMITTANCE
LUST CASSETTES
```

71

```
LATE CLAMPS WAS
ERST HAWAII APE
IMPEDIMENTA POL
 RUDEST MAILS
SEINE INEPTLY
PANELDISCUSSION
ACT ETC TEE
THOU CDROM SASS
 NEO AVE SHE
ELECTROMAGNETIC
AIMLESS ALIAS
RACER PANAMA
FIE NARCOLEPTIC
USE ANEMIA SERA
LED LAYERS EDEN
```

72

```
 BAGDAD RECOUP
BERMUDA ERRATUM
REDTAIL PROTEGE
I U LEA ASPER R
GPO USSR NINE
HOUSE IOTA NIL
TISHRI RECOVERY
S UNDECEIVE V
TOILSOME DELTAS
INN LARK RAINY
PSST CYAN GAS
T TORSI ROD H T
ODONATA SHEATHE
PARAPET TIEBEAM
 DELETE STRAND
```

73

```
B A H A M A S ■ L A W L E S S
O C A R I N A ■ U S A ■ P I P
R E S E N T S ■ B E R N I N I
S ■ T ■ I S O B A R ■ T E N ■
C E A S E F I R E ■ A ■ O D E
H A T H ■ R E T R A N S M I T
T R E A T E R ■ S U T T E E S
■ ■ R O E ■ ■ ■ T O R ■ ■ ■
S C H E R Z I ■ F O R E S E E
C R E S C E N T I C ■ A P E X
H E R ■ H ■ D E T R I M E N T
L E O ■ I G U A N A ■ L ■ E
E P I G E A L ■ E T A I L E R
P E N ■ R U G ■ S I L V E R N
P R E C E D E ■ S C L E R A S
```

74

```
A G R O U N D ■ T S P ■ S H E
H U E ■ S U R F A C E M A I L
A T S T A K E ■ M A R A N T A
■ T O O ■ E S C A P I S T ■ T
H A R N E S S ■ B E D ■ A T E
O P T E D ■ E E L ■ O F F E R
D E S P O N D ■ E S T E E M S
■ R ■ O ■ E ■ ■ O ■ L ■ P
E C H E L O N ■ E N C O R E S
C H Y M E ■ E O N ■ A D O R E
L A M ■ G A G ■ F O R E S A W
A ■ N A R R A T O R ■ S E T
I R O N O U T ■ R I D E O U T
R A D I O B E A C O N ■ I R A
S T Y ■ M A D ■ E N A B L E R
```

75

```
S C U T T L E S ■ A D V E R B
L O N E S O M E ■ D U E L E R
U N C A P P E D ■ I D E A T E
N E A R ■ ■ R U P E E ■ B R A
G Y P ■ ■ F I C H U ■ C O A T
■ ■ ■ F E L T E D ■ ■ A R C H
S A B O T E U R ■ R E L A T E
T R A N C E S ■ L E G A T O R
E A R T H S ■ T A N G I E R S
A G R A ■ ■ B Y P A S S ■ ■
M O I L ■ P U P I L ■ ■ D E N
I N S ■ L U R I D ■ ■ V E L A
E I T H E R ■ C A P S I C U M
S T E E V E ■ A R E A C O D E
T E R R O R ■ L Y N X E Y E D
```

76

```
S O L V E R S ■ D E L O U S E
T R I A D I C ■ U S U R P E D
E L G R E C O ■ N A M E T A G
R A H ■ N E O ■ C U P ■ O D E
O N T O ■ S T Y E ■ S O P O R
I D E A L ■ S A C S ■ N A G S
D O N K E Y ■ K A I S E R S
■ ■ ■ G E M ■ P A N ■ ■ ■
■ B I P O L A R ■ M O D E S T
S I G H ■ P L E B ■ B U R K A
T O N I C ■ A V E R ■ G R I P
A D O ■ H E M ■ D A B ■ A P E
T A B L E A U ■ A D A P T O R
A T L E A S T ■ M I S S I L E
L A Y E T T E ■ N O T I C E D
```

77

```
D S A ■ B A P ■ W O E U N T O
I A S ■ I L I ■ A V E N G E R
S N A S H E S ■ V I R G U L E
L I F T ■ F T S E ■ O N E R
U T E R O T O M Y ■ G R I S E
S I T A R ■ L A S I N G ■ ■
T Z I G A N E S ■ N U D I S M
R E D ■ E T H Y L ■ N T A
E R A S E R ■ E P A N O D O S
■ U C K E R S ■ F L I C S
K O M B U ■ P O I N T L A C E
I P A D ■ H O L I ■ A N A T
L A R I D A E ■ O F F S I D E
P R O V E R B ■ I T U ■ S O R
S T R O O K E ■ D Y N ■ E S S
```

78

```
B A G H D A D ■ C U P F U L ■
U P R E A R ■ ■ D R O P ■ B
S P A M M E D ■ A D O P T E E
T E N ■ S T R I P E D ■ O R R
L A I C ■ E A R T R U M P E T
E S T O P ■ W E E ■ C O A C H
S E A W A L L ■ R E T O R T S
■ ■ P S I ■ ■ G I N ■ ■
A T T E S T S ■ F O O L I S H
C R E A M ■ A T E ■ N I C H E
C O N S U M M A T E ■ T E A R
E M S ■ S U B T E X T ■ D I M
S P E C T R A ■ S T R E T T I
S ■ S U E R ■ ■ R E S E A T
■ S T E R E O ■ C A F T A N S
```

79

```
■ E D I S O N ■ C A R E S S ■
S N A T C H ■ T H R U S H E S
C O N S U M E ■ E B B T I D E
I R K ■ D ■ W Y L I E ■ N A N
O M E N ■ B E A S T ■ A N T I
N O S Y P A R K E R S ■ E E L
S U T L E R S ■ A A H E D ■ E
■ S ■ O A R ■ G O A ■ G
S ■ U N T I E ■ S E A S T A R
T E N ■ S E R I C U L T U R E
E X I T ■ R E C U R ■ S I D E
A C T ■ A R C E D ■ I ■ T E D
D E A D S E T ■ S A R D I N E
S P R U C E L Y ■ C O N O I D
■ T Y P I F Y ■ Z E N A N A
```

80

```
S M A S H U P ■ U P T O P A R
M I S C E L L A N E A ■ O V A
U N H A R N E S S E D ■ T O T
G ■ D E A D P A N ■ P A C T
G N P ■ ■ G ■ F ■ E T A L
L O O M ■ X E B E C ■ N O D E
E N L A C E ■ A ■ R A N C O R
■ R A D ■ N I S E I ■ A R P
M E R I N O ■ R ■ M O N I E D
I S I S ■ N A A C P ■ T S A R
L I M O ■ T ■ H ■ ■ P R Y
A D E N ■ G O N E B A D ■ N
G E T ■ D E N U M E R A B L E
E N E ■ U N A N I M I T I E S
S T R U D E L ■ C A L E N D S
```

81

```
A E G I S ■ E D D A ■ S T A B
S P U N K ■ N A I F ■ T O L U
P E N C I L S H A R P E N E R
S E S A M E ■ ■ D O L L A R S
■ ■ ■ P A S T E ■ Y A L T A
O T I C ■ ■ O H M S ■ ■ ■
N O T E C A S E ■ T O E C A P
C O L D B L O O D E D N E S S
E N L I S T ■ R E M E D I E S
■ ■ ■ O P E C ■ S L A T ■
A D A P T ■ S M O T E ■ ■
B I L L O W Y ■ ■ A R C I N G
B O T A N I C A L G A R D E N
E D E N ■ T H I S ■ S A L S A
S E R E ■ H E R D ■ E G E S T
```

82

```
. F O G . F R E T . Y A W N
D R U M . L I N E . E R R O R
R E S T . E N D S . N E I G H
A Y E . G A G . T A T . T O O
B A L S A . . . N A N . . .
. . A S H . D A Y . U G L I
T I L E . E M U S . N O O K
A C E . R E C C E . A G O .
L A V A . N A I L . A D E N
C O I L . H U T . K I N . .
. . L E I . . . . O T T E R
O R B . E M U . K E N . A L E
C O R E R . S L A V . B R A N
A L I B I . P A Y E . R E T D
. L O B E . S O O N . O D E .
```

83

```
U N S E A L S . A T T E S T .
S O M A L I . . W H E T . O .
E M E R A L D . D E R N I E R
L A T . R A P T U R E . P R Y
E D A M . C H I C K E N P O X
S I N A I . I C E . P U L S E
S C A N D A L . S O I R E E S
. . N E T . . . . R E S . . .
R A P I N E S . D E C E A S E
E V E N T . A P R . E R R O R
G I N G I V I T I S . Y A L E
R A N . F I N A N C E . B U M
O N A N I S T . K U W A I T I
W . M E E T . . . T E R C E T
. D E O D A R . C A R C A S E
```

84

```
A S I A N . B O S S . U R S A
R O B L E . I N C A . S E A L
E R I C A . D U A L . E V I L
A B S O R B . S L O B . E G O
. . . H E R S . P O O R L A W
M E N O R A H S . N A Y . . .
I D O L . G O O F . T E R M S
C G I . G A L A H . . E O N .
E Y R I E . L E G O . A S T I
. . R A F . D O O R S T E P .
K N E E C A P . T H A I . . .
E A R . H U R L . A N N A L S
Y U A N . L O O M . G I G U E
E R S E . T B A R . E N U R E
D U E T . Y E N S . R E E K S
```

85

```
H A R M . T I P I . . E M I R
E X H I B I T I N G . G E N E
N E E D L E S S L Y . O R C S
. S A W E R . H A M S . C U T
. . E A S T . I S O B A R . .
R O G E R . O L D . C O N . .
A M O K . E R A . P L A T T E
J A R . B R I T T L E . I R K
A N G L E R . H A Y . G L E E
. O A F . H E R . B R E E D .
. I N V O K E . O S L O . . .
A D Z . G E L D . M I T T S .
L Y O N . P I A N O S T O O L
O L L A . T O N I C S O L F A
E L A N . . S A L K . S L A B
```

86

```
M O O S . . S P A . R I S C .
A R C H . I L E X . R O D E O
N E A R . B U R L . A M O N G
N O S E P I E C E . M A L T .
. . W A D D Y . W I N . . . .
S M U D G E . T R E L L I S .
T A N . E M P L O Y . A U T O
A C R I D . O E R . O W N E R
C H I C . E D I T O R . G M T
K O P E C K S . O B S E S S .
. . W E E . M E D I C . . . .
. D U A L . P O O L T A B L E
F O R T E . R U S E . R O I L
D W E E B . I S I S . E L L S
A D A R . M E N . D A T E . .
```

87

```
A B E T S . E L M S . P L A T
L I N U M . N E A T . L A D E
P O S T A L C O D E . A C H E
. . C U R I A . . . E S T E E M
A G O . T E M P E R A T U R E
P E N S . P O I . L E P E R .
R E C I P E . U R E A . . . .
. Z E R O T O L E R A N C E .
. . . M A D E . E M E R G E .
O S T I A . O N E . W A G E .
T H U N D E R C L A P . N Y C
T A R G E T . U N I T E . . .
A M B O . U N F A I T H F U L
W A I T . D I E T . T U L L E
A N T S . E P E E . A D Y T A
```

88

```
O D D . S C R E W E D . T I P
D U O . A H E M . A E R A T E
E S P . C O P S . T H E I S T
. T A I L O R . S I N . . . .
S U N R I S E . P O S T W A R
U P T A K E S . L U C E R N E
B . . E Y E W A T E R I N G .
O V A . N A G . . . T E A . .
R I C K E T T S I A E . . L .
N O M I N E E . O B V E R S E
S L E D G E D . C R E W E L S
. . D A N . . L A R E D O . .
O R T E G A . B A D E . E G O
T U A R E G . U S E S . Y A W
T E N . D E S S E R T . E N E
```

89

```
W A D I . O G I V E . A P E S
E B O N . B E L I E . H O R N
B E S T S E L L E R . I L I A
S L E E P Y . S W I M M I N G
. . R O S A . . E A S T . . .
G U A N O . N O D . R A I N S
U N D E R I N V E S T . C A P
T I M E . D E U C E . S K U A
T A I . G O A L K E E P E R S
A T S E A . L E E . S E D U M
. . S M U G . D A T A . . . .
D R I B L E T S . V E R S U S
R O B E . N E T H E R M O S T
A U L D . O N A I R . E L S E
G E E S . A S Y E T . N O R M
```

90

```
. B L E A T S . H O T R O D .
F R A N C E . T A B O U R E T
R O W D I E S . T S U N A M I
E N S . D . E L E C T . T A R
S C U M . S N A F U . N I N A
C H I A R O S C U R O . O D D
O U T L I V E . L I N E N . E
. S . A C E . . . T S P . D .
H . D Y E R S . S I E R R A S
E G O . S E E E Y E T O E Y E
A L U M . I R O N S . M A T S
R E B . A G I N G . Z . D O T
S A L E R N O . E P I S O D E
E M E R I T U S . S N A P A T
. S T R A Y S . N I C E T Y .
```

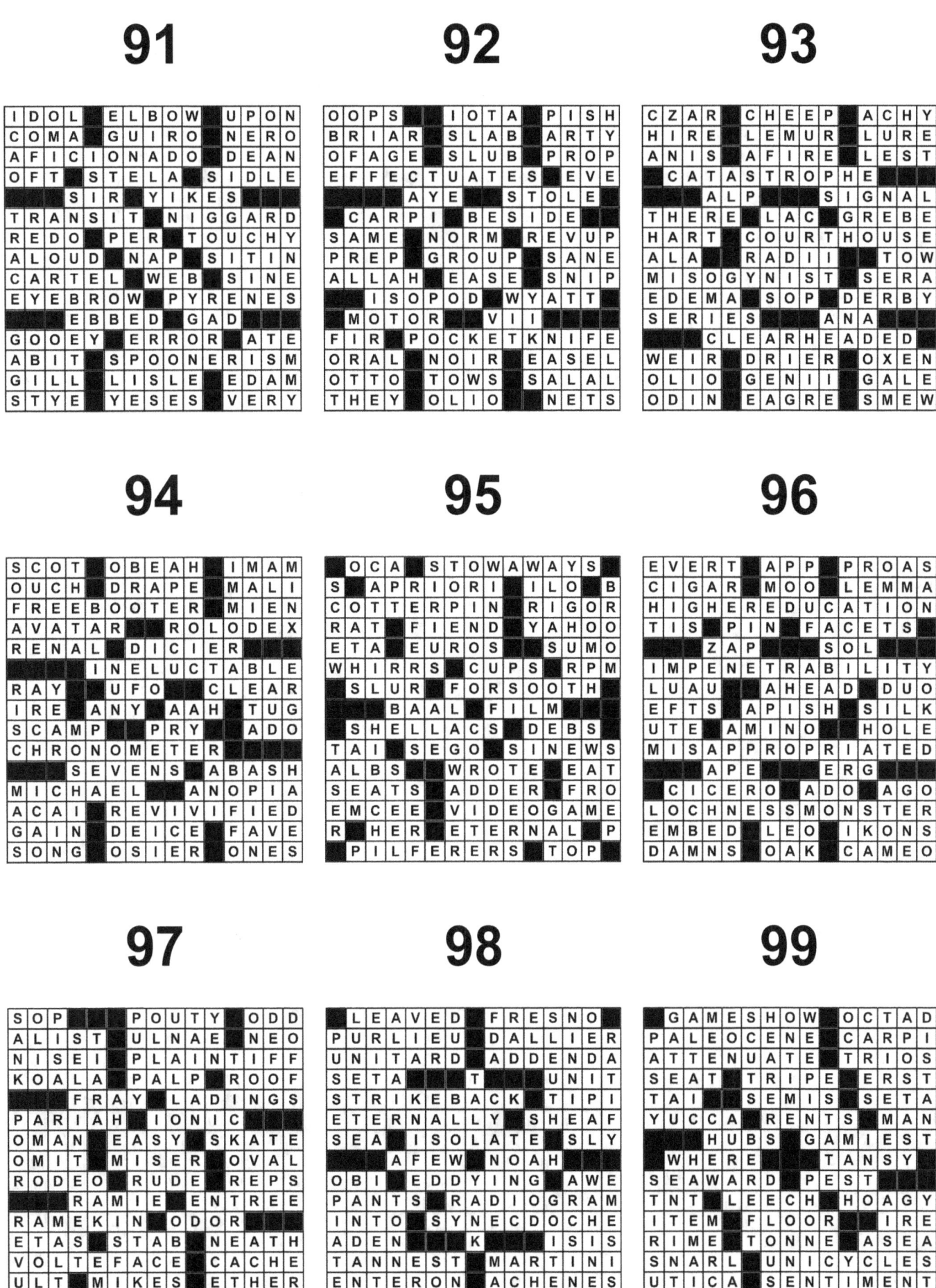

100

101

102

103

104

105

106

107

108

109

110